LOVE AND HUMAN REMAINS

poems

by

R. N. TABER

"Colour, creed, sex, sexuality…these are but part of a whole.
It is the whole that counts."

First published in Great Britain in 2000 by Assembly Books, C - Hammond House, 45a Gaisford Street, London NW5 2EB

All rights reserved. No part of this publication may be reproduced, stored in any retrieval system, or transmitted in any form or by any means, without prior permission from the author.

ISBN: 0 9539833 0 7

Typesetting, layout and cover design: ProPrint, Riverside Cottages, Old Great North Road, Stibbington, Cambs. PE8 6LR

Copyright 2000

KINGSTON UPON HULL CITY LIBRARIES	
54072003138488	
Browns Books	23/03/05
ANF	13.50
821.914	

DEDICATION

ARTHUR ATKINS
(1873-1899)

Spirit of Liverpool, burning bright,
like autumn leaves in the glare of day;
Sombre, in twilight - kaleidoscope
eternal;
Candle holder, seeking here and there
all the naked eye cannot see;
Visions of the mind, across
infinity;
Braveheart, ventures to France, Italy,
exploring paths of creativity,
imploring the soul
a native anxiety;
Bursts upon a New World society
chasing gold tales. Let love, art
and poetry leave their
own trails;
To the landscape of a land
in its flowering youth - the lonely,
lively passion of a pilgrim
seeking truth;
Life, snuffed like a candle by Nature
left unmoved, even by devotion;
Persists, the subtle flame - of
a painter-poet's passion...

in each tawny leaf that falls, among
crowded Piedmont hills

Note: William Arthur Atkins - known as Arthur - was an English artist, raised in the Liverpool area. He studied art in Paris but never exhibited in Europe. His paintings were frequently on show in the San Francisco Bay area of California before his death at the age of 25. One of a group of painter-poets responsible for *The Lark*, an arts magazine published in the San Francisco area during the late 19th century, this remarkable young man has been an inspiration to me. His grave overlooks the same Piedmont hills he loved and painted, although now encroached upon by urban spread.

CONTENTS

PART I: NATURE STUDY   1

View From A Church Window (1984)   2
Time On Haworth Moor (1984)   3
Dog Roses (1991)   4
To A Sunny Day (1979)   5
Dreaming Suburbs (1980)   6
Snake In The Grass (1974)   7
The Visit (1977)   8
A Colouring Book (1998)   9
Stormy Weather (1992)   10
Overkill (1976)   11
Time and Tide (1976)   12
Shell Seekers (1991)   13
The Inheritors (1973)   14
A Seaside Calendar (1984)   15
Shore Leave (1979)   16
Riders Of The Watch (2000)   17
Shades of Hamlet (1984)   18
Nature Study (2000)   19
Past Imperfect (1998)   20
Railroaded (1998)   21
Paradise On Hold (1999)   22
Pantomime (1974)   23
Harvest Home (1999)   24
Once More, Dear Friend (1985)   25
The Music Lovers (1978)   27
A Long Walk By The Sea (1999)   28
Holiday Romance (2000)   29
Halfway To Heaven (1970)   30
Dark Side Of The Sun (1993)   31
Ghosts (1991)   33

Dummy Run (1997)	34
Clouding Over (1997)	35
Caveman (1974)	36
Brush Strokes (1974)	37
Ancestral Voices (1999)	38

PART II: URBAN SAFARI   39

A Roman Walks, 21st Century (2000)	40
This, My City (1985)	41
Rush Hour (1991)	42
Street Art (1998)	43
A Tale Of Two Cities (1972)	44
Some Statistics Wear Sneakers (1980) [i]	45
Funeral Rites (1993)	46
View From A Bridge (1974)	47
Sunrise, Sunset (1997)	48
Ritual Slaughter (1990)	49
Night Spots (1980)	50
Rites Of Passage (1995)	51
Pisces Rising (1996)	52
Poetry Live (1976)	53
Otherworld (1990)	54
On The Counter At Hamleys (1974)	55
Climbers (1999)	56
Closed Circuit TV (1998)	57
Observations Of A Fat Cat (1972)	58
Neighbours, 2000 AD	59
New Kids On The Block (1996)	60
Junkie (1971)	61
Life Class (1976)	62
King's Cross For The Northern Line (1996)	63
Urban Safari (1985)	64
999, Which Service? (1998)	65
O, Cervantes (1972)	66

Hidden Persuaders (1978)	67
About The Size Of It (1997)	68
Bedsit Lifer (1979)	69
Bringing Home The Bacon (1998)	70
A Canterbury Tale (1996)	71
Citizen 2000 (2000)	72
City Farm (1997)	73
A Good Bash (1991)	74
Generation Giro (1998)	75
Graffiti Run (1998)	76
Through A Glass Darkly (1984)	77
PART III: ALT-CTRL-DELETE	79
The Hanging Man (1974)	80
The Raid (1996)	81
A Long Walk To The Job Centre (1994)	82
Lines On The Death Of A Soap Hero (1980)	83
Alt-Ctrl-Delete (1998)	84
A History Lesson (1993)	85
Joker (1974)	86
Alter Ego (1976)	87
At Risk (1993)	88
Armchair Theatre (1972)	90
Circumnavigating Homer (1972)	91
Child's Play (1977)	92
Calling Home (1999)	93
A Ghost Story (2000)	94
A Feeling For Crosswords (1984)	96
Gulf War (1990)	97
Last Rites (1999)	98
Depressed Of Erewhon (1997)	99
Conversation Piece (1976)	100
Diary of An Egg (1997)	101
A Feeling For Carbuncles (1999)	102

Olympic Games (2000)	103
Rogue's Gallery (1980)	104
See How They Run (1999)	105
To Apollo, Over (1974)	106
Tripping (1977)	107
Trainspotting (1983)	108
Window Dressing (1981)	109
Ulysses, After Prime (1972)	110
Wake (1975)	111
Whatever Happened To Once Upon A Time? (1996)	113
Endgame (1970)	114
Systems Failure (1999)	115
Alarm Call (2000)	116

PART IV: AUGUST AND GENET — 117

Growing Pains (1990) [ii]	118
Coming Out (1987)	119
Ordinary People (1985) [iii]	120
Chance Meeting (1998)	121
Wasteland 2000 (2000) [iv]	122
August & Genet (1971)	123
Sex, Lies & Stereotype (1995)	124
Sauna (1996)	126
On Hampstead Heath (1990)	127
Well Of Loneliness (1997)	128
A Moral Tale (1985)	128
A Perception Of Pinks (1998)	130
Wish You Were Here (2000)	131
Oscars (1999)	132
Lines On A Friend (1984)	133
I & I (1976)	135
A Close Shave (1991)	136
Rent (1982)	137

Bold Italics (2000)	138
Fly Away, Peter (1979)	139
Family Values (1991)	141
Dorothy Who? (1987)	142
Ebb Tide (2000)	143
Spring, Autumn, Leicester Square (1980)	144
Chat Room Agenda (1999)	145
Between The Acts (1995)	146
Family Ties (1999)	148
Between Friends (1974) [v]	149
Blue Eyes (2000)	150
Awakenings (1985)	151
The Quilt Makers' Song (1995) [vi]	152
Who Dares, Wins (1999)	154
Gay Pride (1996)	155
Hidden Agenda (2000)	156

PART V: LOVE & HUMAN REMAINS — 157

Affairs Of The Heart (1991)	158
To An Express, On Time running (1977)	159
Time Warp (1997)	160
Sunset On A Country Churchyard (1972)	161
Blueprint For A One-Night Stand (1990)	162
Salute To A Prostitute (1976) [vii]	163
Strangers On A Train (1998)	164
Picking Up The Tab (1996)	165
Out Of Season (1970)	166
Night Moves (1977) [viii]	167
Singles (1997)	168
Love Letters In An Attic (1993)	169
The Last Kiss (1977)	170
Love After Death (1976)	171
Looks Familiar (1998)	172
In Remembrance Of Times Past (1999)	173

Love & Human Remains (1997)	174
Home Alone (1985)	175
If Only (1991)	176
A History Of Abuse (1997)	177
The Empty Nest (1998)	178
Halfway House (1998)	179
All Dressed Up And Nowhere To Go (1997)	180
Bus Stop (1993) [ix]	181
Charybdis Mon Amour (1971)	182
A Class Act (1977)	183
Close Friends, Distant Lives (1994)	184
Dance With A Stranger (1994)	185
Director's Cut (1998)	186
Friends (2000)	187
Matins (1996)	188
The Lovers (1991)	189
Legend (1995)	190
Mates (1998)	191
Daydream Believer (1998)	192
The Longest Journey (1994)	193
PART VI: TRIUMPH OF THE SPIRIT	195
Millennium Dawn (1999)	196
Waters Of the Womb (1998)	197
The Longest Day (1980)	198
Intensive Care (1996)	199
Triumph Of The Spirit (2000)	200
Classroom Politics (1999)	201
Pilgrim (1985)	203
Postcards From Berlin (1991)	204
Buried Alive (1977)	205
Body Positive (1990)	206
Pottery Class (1973)	208
Riches In The Clay (1999)	209

A Phoenix In Soho (1999)   210
Wishful Thinking (1977)   211
Universal Soldier (1999)   212
Refugees (2000)   213
Heaven Can Wait (1998)   214
Braveheart (2000)   215
Resurrection (1976)[x]   216
In A Word (1999)   217
Surfing (1970)   218

PART VII: A CHRISTMAS CAROL   219

Christmas At The Going Rate (1997)[xi]   220
Chasing The Dragon (1986)   221
Angel Watch, 2000 A.D. (1999)   222
A Christmas Carol (1997)   223
Walking the Dog (1999)   224
Crisis At Christmas (1993)[xii]   225
An Ulster Carol (1994)   226
Christmas Comes But Once a Year, If Only! (1997)   227
Advent Calendar (1990)   228

[i] Originally published as *To A Statistic* in *Inner Feelings*, ed. Mark Magee, Book Mark Pubs. 1997.

[ii] Slightly revised version of a poem of the same title in *August and Genet* by R.N.Taber, Aramby Publications (Wire Poetry Booklet 12) 1996; first published in its present form by Community of poets (Canterbury) Winter 1999

[iii] Slightly revised version of a poem of the same title in *August and Genet*, 1996; *Visions of the Mind*, Spotlight Poets, 1998; Forward Press Top 100 Poets of the year vol.1, 1999

[iv] Revised version of *Tiresias Out of The Wasteland* in *August and genet*, 1996

[v] Revised version of *A Visitation* in *August and Genet*, 1996; first published in its present form in *Time Flows By*, Poetry Now, 2000

[vi] Originally published as *Pride* in *August and Genet*, 1996; first published in its present form in *A Search for Truth*, Poetry Now, 2000

[vii] Slightly revised version of a poem of the same title in *August and Genet*, 1996; Wire Poetry Magazine Issue 10, 1997

[viii] Original title. Published as *End Of An Affair* in *A United Voice*, Poetry Now, 1999

[ix] Slightly revised layout of a poem of the same name in *Peer Poetry Magazine, April* 1997; *Superfluity*, Issue 1, 2000

[x] Slightly revised version of a poem of the same name in *How Can You Write a Poem When You're Dying of AIDS?* ed. John Harold, Cassell, 1993

[xi] Originally published as *Home for Christmas* in *Christmas Past*, ed. Mark Magee, Book Mark Pubs. 1997; first published in its present form by Community of Poets (Canterbury) Winter, 1998

[xii] Slightly revised version of a poem of the same name in *August and Genet*, 1996

Part I

NATURE STUDY

VIEW FROM A CHURCH WINDOW

There's a thrill of blossom
on the old tree,
a greeny-white chirrup of noise
bouncing gently, like
a ball in child
hands

Every nuance of creation
about the old tree
tuned to perfection; you and me
shaking our heads at confetti
coming down like
acid rain

A hymn to life,
such beauty!
Tiny wafers of noise
tongued lightly
at the kissing gate
over there

Here, a dim view
of immortality
as we pass our seasons by
grown deaf
to each
leaf

TIME ON HAWORTH MOOR

Sun on the moor
as lovers kiss, stir a music
of hearts
words cannot contain;
Mist on the moor
as lovers tryst, seal the lyric
to an old magic, snails
under stones

Wind on the moor
as love's moods give the lie
to that old dare - stones
shall not weep;
Rain on the moor
as lovers fret at separate
windows - seeking words,
world shut out

Snow on the moor
a lover's grave stirs
a lonely passion
no words could save;
Sun on the moor
mocks us all, we thralls
of Time - gives
a snail heart

DOG ROSES

Dog roses at the crossroads,
twin journeys begin;
A scent of wild desire
smouldering within
each savage breast
despairing rest

Choices to make, promises
to break

Dog roses filling our senses
in a manner of times past;
Catching up the moon,
sun setting fast,
teasing our desire,
fire with fire

Choices delayed, promises
put aside

Dog roses at the crossroads,
twin journeys begin;
A scent of wild desire
smouldering within
each savage breast
despairing rest

Wild dogs of spring, forgiven
us nothing

TO A SUNNY DAY

Little birds singing on the garden wall

>I'll not write you up
>you're too sentimental
>for the Age, they say

As one to another you brightly call

>I'll shut the window
>there's a good film on
>TV today

Silvery sunlight casting cameos everywhere

>making all our
>screen faces
>disappear

Close the curtains, son, better already

>now we can really
>see what's going
>on

DREAMING SUBURBS

Daylight fading at the window, thrushes
singing at will;
Thoughts turn the mind slowly
like sails of a windmill;
Twilight dips a darker hue
(One thrush soars, another stays
to sling its shadow among
the best geraniums);
Melody, fading. A flickering of feathers
at the sill;
Though darkness drop its shutters
on all the world's sleepers,
candles lit for a Quixote surely will
guide a thrush to its nest,
let weary heads rest, having
done their best? (As for dreams,
finders keepers)

Gone now, sweet songbird;
Nothing's heard but sails in the wind
teasing mankind

SNAKE IN THE GRASS

Thin thread
of moonlight
trickles down a hill
loops a bush
jumps a ditch
wriggles under a hedge
reaches a lane
where feet are stamping
stops at a breast
grown tired
of waiting

THE VISIT

It ought to be raining
for a walk in the cemetery
dark and sinister
shadows pricking the neck
cold fingers numbing;
But the sky is clear
as I peer at heads smelling
grassy, spread neatly,
sunning long faces.
Here lies - can't make you out,
Might be, or might not.
Can't see, must be
raining

A COLOURING BOOK

Blue, the colour of a morning sky;
Golden the sun, risen high;
Green, the grass where lovers lie
and let the world rush by
without a care

Blood red, crushed poppies
in their hands, like
a fallen soldier's wounds
and barely a skylark
left to mourn

Silvery grey, dusk's pall.
A pattern of sapphires
emerging - love and death
converging on
us all

STORMY WEATHER

Cloud faces grimace
Lifelines leafing
Through the rain
Fantastic canvas
Leaping at the eye
Rooftops dripping
Sweat of heaven
A rhythm of children
Braving a temporary
Freedom

A rush of images
As ever seen
Van Gogh, Jarman
Each to their own
Inspiration
Distant threats rumbling
Our fears in passing
While, reprieved
We pass it off
As living

OVERKILL

Gone, the meadow
once we met and trod
daisies underfoot;
Shades of grey
looking up, no sign
of redbreast;
A blur, the M-way's
progress (short cut, to
madness);
Grim, the daily
funeral procession
for cock robin

TIME AND TIDE

*The lonely sea laps at my feet
the starry sky comforts
not*

I linger on a hushed beach
a huge white moon
winks at me

Sun, sea, sand
turn in my
hand

Life, death, love
hover low
above

The wind is getting colder.
I am getting
older

Night-pools swirl around me
surprise, confound
me

Even as I stand, on this
passionless shore
I know

*Why the lonely sea laps at my feet,
why the starry sky comforts
not*

SHELL SEEKERS

No harder thing I do than loving you
at a distance as of sea and sand
at the going out of each tide,
at each coming up of the sun,
all the colours of morning strung
like prayer beads across the sky,
a benediction! You and I
as footprints on the shore;
Together. Parting. Wiped out.
Another tide, another morning,
another day - someone's searching
who'll know that we were here;
Beyond time and space,
false perimeters of place,
our love well-preserved
nor finer served than
by a shell's poetry, as
restless as the sea,
deceptive as each dawn

Like prayer beads, to
each our own

THE INHERITORS

Man discovers diamonds
in the sand, gathers them up
in a greedy hand;
Breeze blows the fortune
in his face

Poets reflecting on diamonds
in the sand, count them out
in the palm of a hand;
Clouds hijack
the lot

Lovers dream of diamonds
in the sand - our tears,
a scalding brand;
Come dawn,
we're gone

Children play with diamonds
in the sand, a pirate's
wonderland;
Treasure for
keeps

A SEASIDE CALENDAR

Laughter, freed on summer-scented air
bursts on jaunty wing;
Glad eyes shine the dipping gull,
excite twin waves – returns
excelling. *Sun on sand,*
O world on hand
to greet me

Joy but hushed, the autumn year
devours the sky;
Sad eyes shape the dipping gull,
endure each wave – returns
excelling. *Sun on sand,*
O world on hand
to greet me

Hopes reviewed, wintry ways
break their silence;
Bright eyes applaud a solitary bird,
brave each wave – returns
excelling. *Sun on sand,*
O world on hand
to greet me

Comings, goings, to'ings, fro'ings
in playful flight!
Wide eyes consume a mating pair,
glide twin waves – returns
excelling. *Sun on sand,*
O world on hand
to greet me

SHORE LEAVE

Grow old, old along with me
who once dreamed, dreamed
of better days...
Soon, soon to be replaced
by some eternal scheme
with time-stitched seam
for the inevitable rat
to nibble at;
Waves, dashed against the shore;
Castles, no more
than a loss of child hours
nor hint of whose footprints
lead our destroyers;
So, reproach the harrying shore
and be sad - or dig in;
Be glad for a castle or two
before high tide catches up
with you, where the cliffs
clash with the sea, over
a common inhumanity

RIDERS OF THE WATCH

Moon shadows, riding white horses
across rippling plains
of dark despair;
A dashing of hooves,
indelible imprint
on the soul;
Ghost riders, deceit
and lies - eternal
goal;
Shivering, waiting…
wanting to run - but
where?
Stripped bare
of a lifetime's
audacity;
(Time to try out
the trappings
of integrity?)

Waves, a crashing ovation!
Moon shadows, a force
for salvation

SHADES OF HAMLET

Time, time! A shifting, sifting play
on love and death - warring, scoring,
giving and partly giving;
Urges better things, tugs at lesser
strengths. All finer struggle
caught in underflow

Now, sun in the water dazzles me
a splendid heaven! White dove circling
saintly, dives on a crumb;
Now, willows weeping for each star fallen.
Ebb tide, grieves
me home

Home, home! A shifting, sifting play
on love and death - warring, scoring,
giving and partly giving;
Urges us to better things, tugs at lesser
strengths. All finer struggle
caught in underflow

NATURE STUDY

Brightness falling from the sky, like
summer rain, makes the flowers grow
and the world shine like rainbow trout
on a school kid's line at a local stream
who should be in the football team
but his dad beat him black and blue,
ma's laid out on the kitchen floor
and he daren't take a shower

Brightness falling from the sky, like
acid rain, makes the trees cry, as leaves
die like fishes in the sea and specimens
carefully laid out under glass - for
a generation to see how killing things
is a sure sign of depravation
but biology, now *that's*
Education

Shadows like corpses on the ground.
Skylark, a forgotten sound at a spot
where revelations in the clay suggest
a once-busy stream in a world
earmarked for a winning team,
the rest of us neatly laid out
under corporate glass,
victims of abuse

PAST IMPERFECT

Summer haze on a lonely road,
rogue leaves falling one by one
like faces in a Hall of Mirrors
reflecting multiple fractures
of times past, hints of joy
and laughter mangled by tears,
those I have loved and lost
gazing anxiously through my fears;
A naming of parts (success,
achievement) - these heads of mine
turned by the darker side
of love, fulfilment;
Tiny flames licking at the soul,
smouldering reminders
of seasons gone, each one
a touch recalled, half-truths
let fall with a smile;
Familiar faces - rallying
at such times of need as this,
once betrayed with a kiss
and put aside, returning
to accuse one whose burning
ambition brought us here,
fuelling a pyre of purpose-built
paranoia. Trial by fire,
wracked with pain

Memory Lane

RAILROADED

Looked forward to spring

Pause to hear a blackbird sing
on my way to the station;
Nothing but aggravation
on the train (noisy school kids,
commuters skulking behind
bland print, jealous of lambs
glimpsed furtively in fields
rushing by). Lark in a lonely sky
spilling joy for us to share
who can but grunt, glare,
generally abuse each other,
unwilling to acknowledge
a universal freedom as we head
for the prison of our day

Train screams a halt!

A worse madness breaks out;
School bags, briefcases
overspill. Somewhere
a lark

Still

PARADISE ON HOLD

Let spring drift into summer,
Let summer greens turn
red and gold;
Let poets make of seasons
all they find, it's
Nature rules;
(Even poets grow cold
when winter calls
on lonely hills);
Soon, daffodils, in their turn;
Ours, too, if the way
of things be true;
Who knows? For each flower
that grows, its season
comes and goes;
For each seed in the wind,
a sometime threat
to our kind;
Let the world wreak its worst,
the good earth will
do its best;
Let Nature share or even take
away, its time unspoiled
by hours

In life, in death, let there
be flowers

PANTOMIME

On wings of sunlight
glides a sparrow
seeking a friendly
bough

Dwarfed by a passing gull,
it seems to take fright

Watching it soar
into an alien
blue, so tiny
so alone…

Cursed, the gull that lay
enchantment bare!

On wings of sunlight
drops a lark
into a busy
sycamore

And it's on with the show!
Music - and more…

Fickle hearts, clapping
like a sparrow's wings
at a gull's careless
outrage

Whose turn next, for
centre stage?

HARVEST HOME

Dragging the feet, loath to meet
fellow commuters on a daily office beat
punctuated with P-A-I-N (three across,
two down). A job's a job and pays the bills.
Forget the skills of native intention, long
since tailored to global invention - along
lines of political correction, reaping
a brave new worldly convention.
So what price, satisfaction?
No peace of mind, for a start
nor hours enough in the day
to let a good heart
have its way

God's in His heaven, let's not be deceived,
though by our neighbours well perceived
and our children grieve for all we've left
undone. Native instincts, left to drown in
a vale of acid rain - where once
aspired a common grass, let
pass for home

ONCE MORE, DEAR FRIEND

Death, rippling the summer corn
like the stirrings of a child unborn,
wondering in the womb - what
freedom between cage and tomb?
So, I lift my head to a gorgeous sky,
loose a few more dreams, watch them fly
like the tail of a child's kite
flapping bravely against all heaven's might;
Now, barely a flicker, waved out of sight
with tearful eye and puckered brow
the child I was, resuming now
across wintry years to wet an eye
that otherwise might have stayed dry
in the summer air, seeking where it never found,
hurting without a sound,
feasting on the harvest corn,
caged in a breast deprived of rest,
tired of hearing all's for the best,
weary of waiting for waiting's end,
lonely for want of a dear friend
sailing on the summer corn, *free,*
smiling wistfully at me
who's left with a heavy heart
to weather the pain that's let us part,
wounded by your look that says
our world should have been
a better place

Music, murmuring a summer breeze
like a guitar strummed with artist's ease
to lull earth's restless womb
before the breaking of The Storm
that's spreading alarm
among the corn;
I spot a field mouse, or maybe not,
so tiny, quick, soon forgot
and I should hasten my own tread,
the music bursting in my head,
O love, life! Instead…
I'll linger in this summer place
and to the wind I'll lift the face
of one who's glad he came to see
the passing of our history
into such natural beauty
as I'd forgot is no less a part of me
than these shoes badly worn
through a world sadly torn
in two, three, more
by love, hate, war,
famine too, I have to say
as in the corn I kneel to pray
to what or whom I may never know
but, dear friend, I cannot let you go
without thanks for this day
that's let me stay

THE MUSIC LOVERS

Songbird

Warbling delicious nonsense
for Adam to yawn
over on his way
downstairs

Songbird

Spilling noon on lush carpets.
Charlotte, busy
at the flower
bowl

Songbird

Providing conversation for the likes
of poor Fanny, stuck in town
mostly and enjoys
a Day-Return

Lark, thrush?

Oh, pleasant enough
as it comes - but
hardly Mozart
at the Proms!

A LONG WALK BY THE SEA

The sea, the sea! Mocking me
with poems of Love, Peace, Happiness
and a gutsy immortality
I could but guess

At work, even at play
I wore other faces,
hid this one well away
under airs and graces

Then upon my life you came,
began peeling at the skin;
I resisted - never the same
once I let you in

The sea, the sea! You and me
forever, proudly

HOLIDAY ROMANCE

There's a shadow on the sand
that points across the sea
to a distant land - where once
you walked with me,
your hand in mine, our laughter
like spray in a summer breeze,
desire sparkling like diamonds
all around, our joy the key
to such rapturous harmony
of sea and shore as ever seen
by lovers who passed
that way before

Even now, in a holiday crowd
I hear you laughing aloud
as I hoist our flag upon
a castle in the sand, dreaming
of that distant land - where once
we strayed and dared to dream,
each for the other, wage slaves
baying for the moon, knowing
our time together would be
over soon and we saved
our tears till after
I had flown

Shadow on the sand,
2000 years on

HALFWAY TO HEAVEN

I can kiss the sky,
I *can*, I *can*!
The wind in its rush
makes breathless
my heart, though at
the start of this day
my mood was dark, dark;
Now sunlight
all livid around me
nearly blinds me;
A gull's cry minds me
a baby, birth, rebirth;
All life here, a tumult
of sea, sky, friendship
and though ecstasy dim,
come tomorrow…
I am, I AM

DARK SIDE OF THE SUN

I look in the mirror
and think of you, wonder
how you are, on the other side
of Time; recall another place,
a kinder face - and sorrow
disappears, your lips on mine
in the once-again summer
of our years, hearts beating as one,
dark side of the sun;
A cup of tea eases me
into dawn's misty shine;
We share burnt toast,
walk a crooked line
between marmalade stains
on the tablecloth;
A sudden grin as choral din
breaks out (heaven on cue);
The sweetest sounds sift us
through and through;
Suffer me, suffer you,
again, again. So let it rain!
Or shine the world
in half-open eyes;
Come pain, strife!
Tumble me out of this earthy
bed, tell me lies;
Let me turn my head,
and gaze into your eyes,
a better life be ours

Century all but gone, a race
well run; much lost, much won.
Our thoughts, busy winding in
such rare strands as ever came
together. Dare, reach out
for one another at
Will-Be-Done

Dark side of the sun

GHOSTS

Rougher the sea than last we ran
here, laughing on the cliffs,
a spring breeze in our hair;
Less kind the sky than last we kissed
there, bluebells surrounding
a passion brought to bear;
Sweet memory, the wings of a
friendly gull soaring our dreams,
love's rhythm to fulfil;
Such heat to embrace your body
and bold! In the vaults of eternity,
our lives grown cold;
Salty now, the hair across my
face, thinned like the heather
at our special place;
Though huddled in a raincoat, I easily
recall the glad heart
that made me thrall;
Gulls squeal! No melody
but a sure grace, whirling
against storm clouds
like a pattern of lace on
an altar cloth, would have
smothered us both

DUMMY RUN

A good seed scattered
among ploughshares;
Field left fallow
long enough

Guests at a christening
file into church

Scarecrow in a spin
among the corn;
bird droppings, on
a battered cap

Scorn for latchkey kids
like fallout

At harvest festival,
pigeon pie;
Crumbs like petals
in a cemetery

Cries of the homeless
on cloth ears

CLOUDING OVER

Summer, the colour
of old brass;
Our lives, a patch
of rolled grass;
Final gesture of
a watery sun – to
kill us off before
the storm! Come, let's
dry our tears
on tissues the colour
of your shirt

Delicate, like my heart
beating beneath

CAVEMAN

In a damp gloom I wander
sometimes - stumble,
bang my head on sudden stone,
hear a thrash of bats' wings;
Though thoughts take flight
to a world that gloats
above, like bats they soon
yearn, yearn a returning;
Groping for the truth of things,
discover only history,
a gathering of bats - in
some remote cave

Face to the sun, back
to the wind;
Caress long grass,
wild, free!

Suddenly, bats'
wings

BRUSH STROKES

Young girl with daisies in the hair
darts across a greeny field;
Though brooding sheep
keep a sidelong watch
on playful lambs, the merry scene
attracts a frisky foal, prancing
at a boundary fence

Innocence

Young girl with daisies in the hair
glimpses a butterfly, gives
laughing chase;
One tangent wing
at a finger's tip, elusive
happiness - caught
on canvas

ANCESTRAL VOICES

Rise and fall, rise and fall,
whispering waves

Tell of Adam in the Garden,
Samson at Gaza, Clinton
for president;
Tell of Boudicca in warrior
dress, Mother Theresa
and saintliness;
Humanity, body and soul;
History, in a golden
bowl;
Spare me your blushes
softly treading
sky;
Retreat behind veil, mask
for naked come I
to it all;
Let me bathe in the twilight
of half-gods, poised
for photocall

Rise and fall, rise and fall,
whispering waves

Part II

URBAN SAFARI

A ROMAN WALKS, 21st CENTURY

He has a lean and hungry look,
prowls ravaged streets,
preying on the minds
of good men, foetal
between hot sheets,
exposed not to elemental strife
(confined in a straitjacket
of half-sleep);
No rest for the Nightwalker
conspiring against time
to shape the thoughts
of good men, who'll
make a plaintive cry or two,
thrash about with wasted passion
like torn beasts – soon to wake
and assume a quick pose

in time to tip corn flakes
on Caesar's corpse

THIS, MY CITY

City of dreamers tramping the snow,
wondering where to find - more
at least, than left behind

City of dreamers traipsing every street;
Spring in the air! (For all
the homeless care)

Softly, softly, the Dream Makers, through
the Valley of the Kings of Lombard - to
the foot of each man's pyramid

City of dreamers, mobiles in hand,
littering Hyde's green,
once pleasant land

City of dreams, fantastically woven
in smoke trails. Small wonder,
each season fails us

RUSH HOUR

No job, no home, only time
for living, dying

People dashing from a railway station
spare a thought or two for poverty
with growing irritation - as if
a beggar's shame dare wag
the finger of blame in their direction
(a grave misperception, not to mention
a cheek). Oh, what the heck?
Chuck a coin and feel better for it,
just don't let it get to you;
Laugh it off later over a beer or two
(reward for a bad day);
Imagine, having to
live that way!

But some of us have work to do...
Get out of my way

On the steps of St Martin's, watching
the parade pass on, weaving fictions around
folk walking alone, small comfort
in church stone, grimacing at sounds
of laughter above the din - reminders
of a better time. Getting cold, looks like rain;
moved on like a lame pigeon (again).
Fool's gold in the kitty, enough for some chips
and a cuppa maybe - then back to the bash
for some company and a dash
of local colour. Someone pauses
to pat the dog and ask his name;
nice of 'em to spare the time.

STREET ART

Peace on earth, goodwill to all,
daubed in blood, on
a sweat shop wall, where
even shadows play hide-and-seek
whenever officialdom
struts its Happy Hour
upon a stage for have-nots
laid bare to compassion's
well-meaning eye;
(Cry, do-gooders! Ever keen
to provide a better hole
to hide, than compromise
society's better side);
Striking images smudged
by acid rain, fudged
by the well-heeled boot
playing it smart

Street art

A TALE OF TWO CITIES

Something-in-the city, approached
by good-for-nothing in the street,
desperate for something
to eat.

"Please sir, twenty pence?" (Probably lice);
The suave looks away.
One grimy finger on a pinstriped sleeve
and the ruddy face turns grey.

Scuttles into a restaurant shaking his head
(might even have mused on Charity awhile);
Digs into a pocket as he comes out belching.
Beggar youth hovers, a gummy smile.

"It's an ill wind, an ill wind"
mutters Something (blowing his nose);
"French fries, cheap wine next
I suppose."

SOME STATISTICS WEAR SNEAKERS

Hosed out at 3 a.m. from Cardboard Junction
into a grimacing moonscape, dripping
paper skin over uncaring stone;
Never felt so alone, so alone!
But you press on, foot before foot,
pausing now and then to wonder
if some head-in-a-bag's a friend.
Now, studying a shop window
but not for goodies on display,
just to check on whatever's attached
to sneakers aching you away
from all this - or so he promised
(or as good as) that fella in the park
yesterday, the one who looked hard
then dropped his card for you
to pick up or ignore and you spat
and ran off but it wasn't long before
you went back...
A pretty card. An ugly business.
Not a bad life though. Better than this.
(Anything, better than this!)
So what choice? Hear model
in the window shout, *Go for it.*
And what's a body for if not to earn its keep?
(O, what I wouldn't give for a bed to sleep!);
Moon's dying, stars too.
Civilization, coming alive...
But not for you - who threw the card away,
knowing he'll be back today

FUNERAL RITES

At a secret corner
in the heart of town
our shadows flare, now
drag each other down,
lie, convulsed
like a smoky fire,
all glow hid, eyes pricked
with tears; each of us dancing
with our fears in the time
we have left – here!
And who goes there
who'll dare stir our coals
to their final crumblings?
Mumblings of half-prayer,
smouldering glances
like autumn leaves
(Ashes to ashes, dust to
dust) – scratchings
at a bus stop, graffiti
for the curious

VIEW FROM A BRIDGE

I watch the lights of London
dance on the river, recall a time
you danced for me;
Busy river, cruising past
Tower Hill, stirring brave
hearts - for good or ill;
As stars flicker like altar candles
and die - river folk
protest not, only I;
Ah, it was not for me you danced!
Nor has the moaning tug below
time for us either;
Wearily, warily, I'll make my way,
let murmuring half-truths
wash over me

SUNRISE, SUNSET

A dusky web
spreads the town;
Paler moon
looks down on the fly
goings-on
of civilization than
lights up
a beggar's face
window shopping
for heaven, in
Bond Street

RITUAL SLAUGHTER

Hungry. Homeless. No dole.
reads a card beside the begging bowl
outside a busy supermarket;
Red-rimmed eyes, trying to read
the pavement for friendly footsteps
worth a pleading glance for even
half a chance of a cuppa in some
cosy café. Ten pence here, fifty
there, the odd quid; enough to
keep a scarecrow in dog food
and what the heck?

Chatty conversation, hacking
at the neck

NIGHT SPOTS

Broken dolls lying in some park
Broken dolls crying in the dark

In sick elms, a sound of sighings
weird like witches
at a brew

Broken dolls lying in some park
Broken dolls crying in the dark

So fair and foul, fair and foul
glides the moping, groping
owl

Broken dolls lying in some park
Broken dolls crying in the dark

From the charred earth, flickerings
and a rustling of leaves
yellowing

Broken dolls lying in our parks
Broken dolls dying in our dark

RITES OF PASSAGE

Alone at a bar, on
third drink, fourth;
Alone, alone, alone!
Hypnotised by the second hand
of a giant clock moving
on, on, inexorably;
Vaguely aware of voices
in the head saying, doing
believing. And I cannot.
So, another beer instead
before I go (so soon?)
out in the cold, where
it's dangerous to grow old
beneath a basher's moon

Ah, Roman! Lend me your ears
as we pass, or the world's
made of glass

PISCES RISING

Eyes of the fortune-teller swimming
like piranhas in a corn flakes bowl;
Slowly, scarlet curtain rising
on family life;
Pain, strife, love where we can,
all down to God for a poor show
put on by breakfast soldiers
frowning at the clock;
Baby's crying, your turn
(some of us have a living to earn,
not to mention a train to miss);
What, no kiss? A dog's life this,
I'll say! And the devil to pay
for clothes, car, phone;
Alone, or so it seems

Whatever happened
to dreams?

POETRY LIVE

Words

to music, out of words
let the sun rise
in the eyes of that ragged-eared mongrel
curled on George's doorstep
tongue lolling stupidly
nostrils a-smoke

Words

to music, out of words
let carnival hot dogs
substitute for garden scents,
make easier the stink
of slop-outs in
the gutter

Words

out of choc-smeared mouths
in Bank Holiday sunshine;
kids in glad rags spilling
on the streets like bin bags;
shirtsleeves copper
getting chatty

Poetry

OTHERWORLD

Haunts our bars, fading more
into shadows with each clink
of merry glasses - fallen
on deaf ears;
Observes some scrawny punk
chance his luck, dripping
fag ends - into pools
of heavy rock;
Strangers, would-be friends
make a virtual killing
on the floor, crowd
yelling for more;
To an all-night cafe, where
a smoke may well last forever
and a ghost discover
small comfort

ON THE COUNTER AT HAMLEYS

They trample on the flesh,
stampede across the mind,
leave a string of broken dolls
to choke on their dust;
But the Toymaker says
we must be kind
to humans

CLIMBERS

Outside, looking in
on a clothes rack of the skin;
Designer labels demanding
attention; sporting a toothpaste
grin, token companion
of an endemic
prostitution

Devil's own luck
they say (but never
to the face), forever
contriving a place
at the top table, laughing
aloud - alone
in a crowd

Fat cats pawing
each arm, (suckers
for a wicked charm);
Life and soul of the party!
Sweet smell of success
like honeysuckle in
a cemetery

CLOSED CIRCUIT TV

Politician playing religion
with ingenuity, better surety
against ambition than any
privileged immunity;
Religious authority up for
temporal impunity, reassured
of immortality by a tabloid
morality

Eye in the sky, panning
the world, stand-in
for a jealous god

OBSERVATIONS OF A FAT CAT

I watch you crawl
up the wall,
wonder if you
will fall

I watch you spin
a web within
the safe shade you think
you're in

Before you're done,
I'll have my fun,
playing at power,
making you run

NEIGHBOURS, 2000 AD

I heard shadows moan,
saw a black rain fall,
smelled death

on the other side of the wall

I saw a withered branch,
caught an anguished call,
flung it back

on the other side of the wall

Still I hear shadows moan,
feel a black rain fall,
smell death

on *this* side of the wall

I raise a feeble hand,
throw out a lonely call
but - flung back

on the other side of the wall

NEW KIDS ON THE BLOCK

Gone shopping
Kids running wild
Trolley rage mums
All-smiles; try the pub
Dogs everywhere
Kids shooting pool
Dads going spare;
On the pavement
Collide with some kid
On a bike (my fault
Forgot to look!);
Knives out in the playground
Acid in the park
Kids chasing death
For a lark;
Cops in their stride
Let's get even;
Kids on a joyride
To heaven;
Mum's off her trolley;
Dad's on the booze

Angel on the sideboard
Yesterday's news

JUNKIE

heaves across
some patchwork wilderness
all scratched and bled
gibbering invocations
to fawning gods;
shreds of a silk shirt
hang from squint shoulders
denim flesh bends
to crap

emptying of bowels
emptying of mind

hieroglyphics, for
all our monkey wisdom
to work at

LIFE CLASS

Shades of blue
each dawn;
Old guitar player
strikes a chord
or two
for civilization;
Come noon,
imitation Picassos
by the dozen

KING'S CROSS, FOR THE NORTHERN LINE

Vision of sadness
Set in amber,
Lips the colour of blood
Spitting silences;
Watch ripples spread
Across a windscreen;
See a dead man's eye
Throw a wink

A precision madness
On stage, scenes
Played out and paid for
With sweat;
A few tears in the head
For baby left sucking a dummy
And mummy out dancing
At a chance wake

Neon lights, betraying
The leisure business;
Music from an arcade displaying
Contempt enough for art
To make a powder monkey grieve
And children dance on every
Organ grinder's grave
Left unattended

URBAN SAFARI

None but shuddering stones across dead lawns
stretching from mossy rails to graffiti trails
on silent factory walls hear the Traveller
who calls for aid - to ease the burden
Time has laid on back and breast;
No thought of rest, not here, where
occasional dock leaves conspire
a gentler ground than makes this gravel
sound like another massacre;
On, on, playful night! Shedding favours
left and right, teasing the Traveller's
jaded sight. Glimpse, a tiger's smile
where a pile of flowery wire flickers
like a far forest fire; city lights, beyond
mass graves of missing people plucked
from giro queues and left to fend
without a friend for years - their ghosts
not far behind, as panic rears!

Neon daubs, for stars
and paper tigers

999, WHICH SERVICE?

Stood on a corner dripping blood
into pools of moonlight, shape-shifting
like a dream at the edge of a world
teetering on extinction;
Pistols at dawn, a roaring in the ears
like a pride of lions in the last rainforest
demanding - "Who cares?"
War of words in places of distinction,
(Death on the streets a welcome
distraction from making a killing
on the Amazon)

Back to the womb's lonely wait, like
a caged lion expected to perform
till brave lips breathe new life in me,
pages of your history
stuck to mine

Blood on the moon, colour of our skin,
universal question

O, CERVANTES

One commuter risen
at seven, running for train by eight
after ritual peck
on doorstep and warns the kids
not to be late for school;
Arrives for work wearily,
sorts the post meticulously,
checks with his secretary
about what went on yesterday;
Another day done, breaks for tea
well-deserved, our hero heads home
packed like a veal calf
on the continental run;
Turns the key about half-six most days,
picking at supper by seven ten;
sends the kids to their homework,
starts to tell the wife about his own work
(dammit, the mobile again!)
A smoke, a glass of red, soap TV,
(better not mention the ulcer,
scary). No outstanding bills
and never, never a thing
about windmills

HIDDEN PERSUADERS

Come, come isolato into the world again

> Forgive yesterday's noon
> it's toothpaste grin,
> let the culling-glitter
> suck me in?

Come, come isolato into the world again

> Close my ears
> to the jingle-jangle of twilights
> given to celebrate some
> pasteboard heaven?

Come, come isolato into the world again

> Close my eyes
> to those neon gauds that strut
> our streets to make
> a belly hurt?

Come, come isolato – into the world

> And then...?

ABOUT THE SIZE OF IT

Small-time crook,
surprised with the swag;
Battered victim makes
the local rag;
Small-town folk
left mostly in dismay,
can't see the sort of joke
that big-time justice
loves to play

Community service, six
weeks and a day

BEDSIT LIFER

Dawn's dust has scarcely
settled at the chin;
An eccentric din
of streets below
reminds that it's time
to go at it

The world's dirt has scarcely
greased the hair;
A rhythmic rush
of leather gear
pants me here, there
at bald faces

An April dusk has scarcely
brushed the eye;
Bird songs hesitate
like mourners gathered
round a stone, now
trickle away

Answerphone's dead,
cat's in a mood;
Predictably, nothing on telly;
Settle for a take-away,
pirate tape won't play,
call it a day

BRINGING HOME THE BACON

World looking grubby
like dirty laundry;
Folk half naked in the street,
bags under the eyes,
corns on the feet, not making
much sense of life in the pink
gone grey (if the Sundays
have their way). So, where
to turn and who to trust?
Now, there's the rub; politics
like church, an exclusive club.
A drag, making sure all
the shopping's done

Mother of invention,
poor companion

A CANTERBURY TALE

At Christ's cathedral,
knelt to pray
unable to enter, for
could not pay;
Let the rain wash
our tears away;
Come again
and not alone!
Poor, sick, thief
come to grief;
Can't go to church
on a Saturday
or call out the doctor
and the cells
are full;
Lines engaged, again
or answerphone;
Trudge miles in vain
out of office hours,
soup and sympathy
on hand, they say
(like showers on
St Swithin's Day!)
some bread even, lottery
ticket to heaven

CITIZEN 2000

Can't get on a bus, school kids
won't walk half a mile;
Stuck on a train, yet another
points failure;
Arrive for work later than usual,
half the staff rung in sick already;
Start to get things done - and
the system goes down;
Mad rush to meet management
deadline only to learn – yes,
extended again!
No relief, no lunch, long afternoon
and just about ready to make
the Home Run;
Soon, feet up and relax (I wish!)
but family strife, no easy life;
A long walk through streets
paved with History's gold,
feeling old - as youths shout names
about wrinklies who wear
designer frames;
Cyclist hogging the pavement
sends shoppers running for cover;
Resentment boils over, and
I stand my ground;
Cyclist takes a tumble, calls
a copper - who takes my details,
says I'll get a letter and rails
how people my age should
know better...

Peace at last on a quiet hill
as dusk settles on my city;
World without pity - but none
so beautiful;
Kite flier taking on a rough wind
with pride - symbol
of humanity's
better side

CITY FARM

Wolves in the smoke
rearing;
Child in a playground
runs off

*Lambs in a field,
fenced in*

Leaves parting from
a tree;
Lark drops like
a stone

*At the heart's edge,
free fall*

Cherry blossom, like
confetti - soaked
in acid
rain

*Out of our debris,
lark risen*

A GOOD BASH

Curtain roof, cardboard walls,
charity sleeping bag, courtesy
of one's social conscience
at surroundings from the dais
or during dinner when pressed
for conversation tactics;
My dear, how awful!
How can people live like that?
One feels so, so...
And did you hear about
Auntie's cat? Such good news
about Jill's promotion
so I suppose it makes sense
to have the abortion;
After all, a job's a job
but a career is class
and, my dear, your glass
is empty, let me refill;
So glad you enjoyed the meal;
Good of you to come
on such a night;
Let's move to the fireside,
forget the fright
outside

GENERATION GIRO

*Drumbeat sounding, forests
of the night*

Sunny days of childhood
clouding up for spite;
Hand up in the classroom,
down for a dunce again;
Ganging up for company
on a wet afternoon;
Banged up with joy-riders,
smashed as the kite
we'd fly in the park
till you got bored
and found other ways
to make your mark, world
running scared, kid
with a blade

*Heartbeat pounding, forests
of the night*

Surrounded by giants;
Pricks of light
in my eyes, forcing tears
for the kite
we'd fly in a breeze
and tease each other
about who pulls the strings
to make us laugh, cry,
make love when we choose,
take chances, lose
everything, prove nothing;
Blade's running red,
kid's dead, enough
said

Silence

GRAFFITI RUN

On the streets, on the dole;
Lost heart, sold soul
for a pair of shoes;
Nothing left to lose
but life itself, gone stale
on the shelf where I doze
by night or day (nothing
to choose between); Death
less obscene than this!
Freak show for tourists,
kick-about for well-heeled
ratepayers, dream photocall
for Opposition molars wooing
the public conscience while
confessing a private disgust;
Smile! Needs must as the Devil
drives. (God's in his heaven
and the Church is on His side
so what harm a spot of benign
publicity in the tabloids?);
Prince looks on wisely.
Pimp doing nicely, thank you.
Fat cats sniffing at the dome
come the millennium

Have-nots under the sun, for
the next Graffiti run

THROUGH A GLASS DARKLY

In a street, tree lined,
children playing hide-and-seek
make din enough
to wake the dead, the old man says
who lives on
the ground floor of an end house
whose shiny steps
such fun we slip, towering wall
a thrill to climb
(by the time he'll rush, no
sign of us!);
Waving a stick, he bawls us out
(we'll mouth him
back, when the door slams shut!);
Children growing up
make no excuses, just din enough
to wake the dead
the old man says, treading
the ground floor
of the end house whose mossy steps
so snug we sprawl,
graffiti wall a joy to lean,
nets a-quiver
at our kissing (or for all
he's missing?)
All change! Children gone.
Traffic enough
to wake the dead, the old man said
who lived that shabby
room, whose crabby gloom
we never spared;
Brave wall, a sorry spread.

Curtains down
(windows boarded up instead).
Ghosts playing
hide-and-seek with eternity
facing a bleak
affinity with wings, for
the last tree
left standing. Mirror, cracks!

A cruelty enduring

Part III

ALT-CTRL-DELETE

THE HANGING MAN

In the shadow of a steeple
I am dangled

All around me
sun-circles swing high,
swing low;
A fear in me starts to grow,
fast risen to the point
of painlessness;
Like the steeple, it pricks
a secret heaven

spilling me

THE RAID

Lark tries to sing
above a din of human voices!
Homes in on a string
of bacon rind hanging
on next door's washing line
to witness a tragedy unfold
like the creases
in a duvet cover, shaken out
by the same kind hands
dragging kids from their beds
as the first cracks
of dawn spread across a lawn
where but yesterday
we came to play until teatime
then ran in out of breath
and, oh, so glad – dad's caught
the early train!

(When will I see you again?)

Screams, tossed
halfway around the world!
But Social Services
have the law on their side
and it makes sense
of a kind, like skylarks
after bacon rind

A LONG WALK TO THE JOB CENTRE

Each way we look, horizons bleak

We scream, cannot speak.
Nothing comes of thoughts of prayer,
unconvinced Someone to care;
Picture a smouldering bush,
watch it flare! Cast grief
into the flame, hear it roar
in the ears, let it die
and tears fall till there's
nothing left but graffiti
on a leafy wall, raging
at a patch of sky; cage bars
too high to heave, where
cloudy faces pause to grieve us
all we might have been
and can't forget, or leave yet
to practice a finer art
but must improve a strategy
for victory over a native
inability to see

Between heaven and earth,
no finer act than rebirth;
a journey through pain
and deprivation, a darker
isolation of fears under the skin
than flaws in our clothes
that we despair but, when
exposed, transcend beyond belief
all we'd pass off here
as a way of life; such things

left unsaid, undone - dear
horizons come and gone!
Clearer now, like altar lace
making peace-trails in the eye;
Defy the Beast! (its pleasures least
drawing us well, well out of reach
once and for all). Who calls?
But a whistling downwind heard long
before a few good men learned
to spell F-R-E-E-D-O-M

LINES ON THE DEATH OF A SOAP HERO

At the clamour of his passing,
stirs good old stand-by, Myth,
in grateful flight (hint enough of life
to succour all-coining minds,
put a TV mandarin on heat);
Couch potatoes fuel the flames,
give the phoenix favourite names,
unaware of spin doctors crouched
behind the armchair – already taken
a lead, slipping a reasoned magic
to even the seasoned cynic;
Given a chance phrase or two (chance
praise?) to promote Dickie Dusters. . .
and we're soon won over;
Let it hover, sweet Bird of Youth,
a truth of alternative convictions;
Myth, indeed, over our
grubby fictions

ALT-CTRL-DELETE

Blank screen staring at me
like a dead man's eye
as if taken by surprise
at the moment of execution,
expecting pulse, heartbeat,
a flow of blood to the works
in spite of those quirks
of human nature that put a body
on hold whenever its world
ceases to turn, civilization
burnt out among the ashes
of personal ambition;
From inspiration, no helping hand
to guide pen or brush;
Desolation, a lush
wading through risen waters
of the earth, baring pain
like a rose its petals
in acid rain, deserving better
at Nature's hand than a travesty
of imitation urged by Man's
jealousy of God

As melting ice caps start to flood
this world of ours, we can lose heart,
drown in its worst nightmares (poet
found dead at the keyboard)
or find a voice

Our choice

A HISTORY LESSON

A, B, C
Candles in the gloom
prick at the mind, tablets
of stone; a dearth of fireflies
jazzing about
here, there

1, 2, 3
Candles blown, fireflies
goaded by a new dawn;
Millennia pricking at
the skin, Socrates
back in prison

Tablets of stone, unclear
for acid rain;
moving fingers
on a rout
found
out

Again

JOKER

You dropped the joke into a humming pool,
let ripples spread
from merry chuckle
to sly whisper

I watched the whisper take its course
from eye to eye
until someone
laughed

Like a freak wave, that laughter came
tumbling upon the whisper,
dashing it to pieces,
scattering me

everywhere

ALTER EGO

On the crown of murdered sleep
leans a grey angel
in martyred pose;
Slope of the head glints redly,
whites of each eye
stare, stare;
One crooked finger hints
at deeds played out
in checkered shade;
Suddenly, descends a snow bird
to tuck this tableau
under wing;
Do I hear a smothered cry,
glimpse again angry
breasting?

The pose, I'll recall, and covert
looks reveal - Grey Angel
knows me too well
for the comfort
of my soul

AT RISK

Toddler in a cave
watching for the giant;
Deaf to the hunt,
coaxes the dog to stay
quiet, sucking
a thumb

Fe fi fo fum

Towers of Babylon
about to fall on me,
crush my world,
transport me to other places
where giants wear
human faces

Fe fi fo fum

I smell blood, creeping
the floor of a cave
and down our stairs
into a world where giants
crave to make a meal
of our worst fears

Fe fi fo fum

Shadows on the wall
poised to spring;
Horns rallying a master race
to cheer Goliath on…
(Game's nearly
up?)

Fe fi fo fum

The dog died in pain,
poisoned by giants;
What's left? Acid rain,
afraid to go home,
hunt's
on!

ARMCHAIR THEATRE

President assassinated,
priest defrocked;
Uproar on the streets
and starvation - all
on News at Ten;
(Your turn to make the tea
then pass the biscuits
round). Terrorists kill,
are killed - in any other name
but their own;
Unemployment's down,
can you believe it?
Ten pounds lottery win,
take it or leave it;
Sleaze politician, facing
difficult choices (school tie
diplomacy come into
its own); Schizo on the run
from murderous voices
(no real sanctuary till
the dirty deed's done);
Love child kidnapped
by its father; M-way baby
for a dead mother;
Another drunk driver goes free,
courtesy of the judiciary;
Local boy done bad, a travesty
of sportsmanship on the field;

Pass me another biscuit
and turn the sound down - so
I can hear what's going on
next door (at it again
I suppose)

Bad news

CIRCUMNAVIGATING HOMER

Charybdis, source of blood-sucking history!
Myth, reaching out to nourish our fictions
at the breast. Eyes of the navigator
burning like twin saints;
Whose lips next shall pluck a kiss from me?
I will suck the life from them, spew out the taste
of them - and Pallas won't care, brave Ulysses
(save Mr Joyce put in a plea, for
the sheer passion of absurdity);
I'll not be cheated of immortality - or
heroes to wrestle the world's straitjacket
while tin gods debate what's right
and what's aesthetic

CHILD'S PLAY

Down at the bread pool,
a solitary swan,
all majesty in tragedy,
no sign of its mate

Who urged the first stone
at Beauty?
Who drank of pink laughter
fizzing?

Crocodile tears, a picture
of innocence

CALLING HOME

Relaxing on the mobile,
bad day at the office;
Looking forward to a long,
hot bath then maybe
a take-away;
(Almost missed the damn turning
off the M-way!);
Good to offload, enjoy
a chat - spot someone
in the road

Too late

A GHOST STORY

I saw a man at the bus stop,
a long time he stood there
but never caught a bus
or ever seemed to care;
Once I asked him - why?
He answered with a smile:
"No need to catch a bus,
I've been dead awhile."

"You're a ghost?" I could but stare.
But his laughter was kindly
and gave no cause for fear;
"I like to meet the buses,
watch folk head for home;
I like to read their faces.
It's like being
alive again."

"It's all there - behind the eyes,
a grin or furrowed brow;
Love, laughter, grief, fear,
like a bag of groceries;
It's the lonely ones who get to me,
our pain just never ends;
So many people - too busy
even for friends."

"You may be rich, poor, famous
or a face in the street...
but I tell you this, for sure - good
friends can't be beat."
I asked him to read *my* face, with
some misgiving. He grinned. "No need.
Who has time for a ghost – should
try it on the living."

I'd been working late
(only losers coast);
I caught the last bus home
after chatting with the ghost;
At the same bus stop,
years on, after a skinful...
I saw a smarter man than me
listening at the wall

A FEELING FOR CROSSWORDS

Uneasy stirs this Muse
in the role of cynic,
tossing and turning
on a hotbed of imagination
like a whore
harbouring more regrets
than she might
care to mention to tabloids
peddling their
shoddy goods to respectable
marmalade men,
fawning up to the cream of
soft soap politicos;
Condemned, watchperson
without humility
for trying to tip the scales of
public judiciary
with a nice touch of private
morality (eyes
down at the Press bench);
Small consolation
for losing out on the lottery;
Contained, the Irish Question
at three across, two down,
on that beastly rush hour train;
Weary, inept, our humanity,
demanding to know whether
life's more than a passing show
put on by over-rated players
dodging Big Brother

who'll drum our young
to war, turn 'em whore,
lay 'em out flat
where Peace strives
a thin, line – between
politics and religion, and whose
the Final Solution?

GULF WAR

Children running hand in hand
oil licking at the sand
woman feeding at the breast
cormorant striving for its nest
missiles screaming through the air
like the ravings of a Hamlet
in deliberate despair
at the world's feet;
World, on the edge of its seat
rooting for baby at the bloody breast
as cormorant almost makes it
to the nest. And our fighting machines
are the very best so the play's soon done;
another big hit, for
audience participation

LAST RITES

Where Mohammed's mountain
touched with gold sweeps down
to a fairytale sea – tales of war
and death are told, torture,
famine, misery...
But a lark sings and a nightingale
(though threatened species)
reminding us of victories
over the darker forces
of Man

Amen

DEPRESSED OF EREWHON

Need to talk to someone
(Unplugged the phone)
Need someone to share
(Won't answer the door)
Can get through the days
But no way out of this maze
Of turnings, yearnings,
Candle burnings to a devil
That drags me out of bed
And plays Pied Piper in my head
Until I join the rat-race;
Need time and space
(None at the office)
Need a hand, an ear
(Look around, where?)
Can't go on like this,
A credit to zombies;
Getting by on auto-pilot
Even when my partner
Turns the light out;
Need to get real
(Take another pill)
Must try, try!
(Just wanna die)

Help me, somebody

CONVERSATION PIECE

not a bad day, so
I've heard say
over the jam

could have been worse;
by the way, I saw a hearse this morning
outside number five

good to be alive!
even in a cactus twilight
that's under the skin

there's a scratching at the door
better let the cat in
I suppose

but before I do
tell me, who else knows
about us?

here we sit, you and I
like figures at that hearse
scratching with each eye

for something to say
after hours
apart

so let's make a start …
what's that? Okay, I'll go
let in the cat

DIARY OF AN EGG

Monday, sat on a wall
contemplating dirty toes;
Tuesday, went to Oxfam
for a change of clothes;
Wednesday, stormed Harrods
on a fantasy spree;
Thursday, signed on late
and copped the third degree;
Friday, had to wave goodbye
a stag night on the tiles;
Saturday, cashed the giro
and paid off some bills;
Sunday, played heaven
at its own game

Humpty Dumpty, jump?

A FEELING FOR CARBUNCLES

At a window looking out
on rain pouring down,
umbrellas blown through,
skids across the road,
flower heads tossed aside
by a wind so cruel it only lasts
awhile - till the sun's return
and God can smile again
upon the damage done
(retribution for pale imitation
at a drawing board, ambition
to change the world – for
a whole generation?);
Ghosts, tracing lifelines
on a tearful window pane,
pausing now and then
only to shrug off a curious
peering in and spurious
moving on

OLYMPIC GAMES

What will be, will be. In this century
as others gone before...
Wealth and poverty, a sick lottery
of love and hate, peace and war
played out by tin gods with humankind
and everything to play for, bearing
in mind that those who dare shall win,
no matter the sin - and losers cast
the first stones than admit
they were taken in, by
substitute icons.

Olympus, on Capitol Hill.
Humanity, in free fall.

ROGUE'S GALLERY

Along checkered paths - beating off
famished eyes chewing on me,
private flesh, disintegrating;
Public faces for the hanging, every one
a statement worthy of fine statesmen.
At half-open windows, smell hyacinth
sucking at my pain. Glimpse grand ghosts
tugging at loud waistcoats. Loosen the tie
(my flag). Mop the brow, sweating out
a bland defence against elected powers
acting up for God in a Hall of Mirrors,
leaving their mark for art's sake (or vanity,
take your pick). Eternity, eclipsed right
here - on Parliament Square

SEE HOW THEY RUN

When Jack was ten, he climbed a tree
and the Fire Brigade was called;
As they got him down, he
played the clown - and
no one liked to scold

When Jack hit sixteen, he helped steal
a car; Old Bill chased after him.
He crashed it bad, a pal died.
Jack did time, a
crying shame

Jack's birthday and ma's done a bake;
a single candle on the cake. Table's laid,
friends and family called - but none
want to know, since he ran off
years ago

Ma's left alone. Dad joins his mates, in
an old drinking song. Wonder, what
went wrong? Did our best for Jack
and he turned his back - what
else to do or say?

Huh, kids today!

TO APOLLO, OVER

Broken statues in the dust
herald an historic
dawn, shoot long
shadows

Far, far the shadows fly
across our native land
like many
arrows

Into a scholar's dugout
one arrow flies, as
this sun
rises

Red sun in the dust
makes broken
statues
bleed

TRIPPING

Let a splotchy sun
throw poppies at me
whose petals pile me high
and I am at one with crickets
in a cornfield;
Ah, but here comes a combine
so let's hitch a lift
from a cocky sparrow
chanced to drop by;
Away, away!
Into Sinbad's territories;
Dangling, ready
to home in

Here, please
set me down here;
(Gently, now!)
Why on earth not?
Oh well, suit yourself
but make it soon
I'm feeling...

Dizzy

No crickets here
or high corn, only skin
and bone - hanging
by a thread

Afraid

TRAINSPOTTING

I heard the engine, the engine
close on me - felt its pulse racing
against mine - saw it pass,
speeding against the clock
(ticks in the brain). Gone now, trailing
a fudge of half-forgotten moments
that rage me still. *Engine, throbbing*
against my will

I saw the wheels, the wheels
rumble me - felt their firings
ghost me - watched them pass, like
raging clocks ticking me;
Gone now, a shimmering maze
of half-forgiven moments
crazing me still. *Wheels, screaming*
against my will

I ride the engine, the engine
pulsing me - share its race
against time. Signals blurring.
Half doubts stoking up. Faster, faster!
Scattering apes from the track,
tearing the poetry off a man's back;
Soul, beyond control - *in*
free fall

WINDOW DRESSING

At a window on my life I gaze,
close my ears to the weary windings
of clockwork days, try to imagine
how it might be should these stiff-neck
streets ever cease their turning me
to what I am - part of this sham
of human boast, comprising toy folk
for the most part though a few
take heart still, tugging at the sleeve
as a child will, anxious to leave
the plastic places and cartoon faces
for see-saw, swings, among other things
we forget soon enough, struggling
to keep some stubborn noon design
intact; part of the same act put on
for each day's passing - to earn
a clapping in the head, come evening
from other toys in the making

ULYSSES, AFTER PRIME

Naked
bold and beautiful
looms she
on a lurid
pea green sea, coming
for me

Bare
shivering with lust
am I
hung out
to dry, with the
washing

Wavings
(wild and lovely!);
Harmless vanity
of a sea dog
rewriting
history

Groans
I'll heave, each
twilight-in-orgasm;
Lament for a hero
tied to a
desk job

WAKE

Away, hideous masks invading a meagre
privacy! Let me rest, let me sleep;
Let me tumble infinite Deep, find
some peace from this turbulence of mind
that's crowding me, urgings as if
God-given. And I am alone, left
to suffer the clumsy hand, the laboured
sentiment. Masks! Mixing us in carnival
at short notice; alas, scarce time
to prepare for the sudden rush of blood
or burnt ear pinned with arm band
to whatever thought appropriate
to wear. Masks! Clowns without a Big Top
spinning us like mother's wool
only, she is gone. And I am alone
to greet the darker side of comedy
with cool kiss here, boiled handshake there,
taking care - oh such care! – not to show
how I long for them to go, just GO,
these hangers-on by a monkey's grin
for the occasion, like ornaments
on a sideboard inviting us all
to indulge in Grotesque (and
with such equanimity), dismissing
even the crass unsuitability
of the hat, the shirt, the lacquered
faces rubbing our dirt. Masks!
Somewhere faintly, thrushes.
Here, sweating out a quality madness
as crooked fingers coax to orgasm
all closet conversation. The poor things
fly off, frightened by this eruption

of humanity from the bowels
of all the world's teacups;
Masks! Let them pass, through the walls
of mother's womb. Let me see
what waits for me beyond this tomb
the clowns have made, so weather
its silences unafraid, before I'm left
passing round the sandwiches;
Masks! Better pick up mine
where I let it fall, and back
to carnival

WHATEVER HAPPENED TO ONCE UPON A TIME?

Fairies in the garden,
dragons in the sky;
Shadowy mists of Avalon
risen high;
Home, some dark cave
in a far, far distant time;
Poetry and heroes,
legends in their prime
come to rescue us from
the terrors of bed-time;
All gone, kids grown
and who's passing on
secrets of protection
to a generation
that prefers computer games
or, better still,
copycat storylines
from Pandora's Box?
(Issues of the day, strategy
in a ratings war. Peter Pan
shot down over Walford);
Beasties under the bed
breaking out like chicken-pox
on a child's face

And no hiding place

ENDGAME

Watch the shadows rise and fall,
seek between and all that's behind,
relax the contours of informed mind;
Wander, trespass, feel your way
through fawning mists of pink and grey;
Behold - all fond Reason left untold.
Caress young visions huge moons have kissed,
meander pathways Time has not missed
only you, dear fool, who thought
you knew it all…

Flames flicker and die. Phantoms fade.
Between gloom and glow, dawn's sly blade
strikes a bowed crown, lets one grey lock
slip slowly d
            o
             w
              n

SYSTEMS FAILURE

If…

Life is a matter of sensibility,
Love a question of values,
Freedom a state of mind,
God what we will

Will we?

If…

We grow numb, or
dumb - behind
a curtain, of
acid rain

Can we?

If…

Rummaging in a broom
cupboard, some amateur
philosopher
may go

So?

Could ask a computer
what IT's all about
but - garbage in,
garbage out

ALARM CALL

Glad chorus greets a dawn
birthing a Brave New World,
poor copy of Eden's
fairer face;
Love in the air, snakes
in the grass - good and evil
sharing our burden
of choice;
Lark, skylark, dear symbol
of light and beauty,
victim of Man's
sheer apathy;
Let us not dwell upon
temptations to sleep on…
but deliver us - from
our own destruction

Part IV

AUGUST AND GENET

GROWING PAINS

It was after Maths and I had forgotten
a text book so you came back with me
to help me look, just minutes to spare
before Chemistry. Suddenly, you
were holding me and your mouth
missed mine only because I panicked
and ran, shoving you aside. I remember
how you cried out, all that fear
and pain and love banging in my head
like passionate drums. But there was
no passion in me, only feelings run riot
and I don't know how I got through
the next weeks, avoiding you at every turn,
demanding of my anguished Youth
other energies to burn, sought
in next-door Mary other lessons to learn
and learned them well, hurled
into a hell of isolation, playing at
boyfriend, bike mate, regular son,
unable to relate to anyone, riding pillion
on Conversation in perfect rhythm
without much sense until, smashed and weary
I let peel off all pretence, layer by layer,
sprawled on my bed, hypnotised by a dippy
moth – making frantic wing overhead

I caught up with you after school one day,
felt foolish fumbling for things to say,
confided a pain with geometry;
You would not even look at me...
At your house you turned the key
just as I found words to chance me

and you gave the door a mighty kick,
blinking back tears that prick me
even now, years on (no idea where
he's gone) and I cherish still
our first nakedness, thrill
to a freedom brought to bear
in ritual ending of our fear

COMING OUT

Like a time-probe your tongue
appropriates me;
I sink into your heat,
burrowing centuries,
bearing my cup - penetrating
layer upon layer of bigotry;
Finally, kneeling at the altar
of our history

I declare myself

ORDINARY PEOPLE

Yesterday, we came to tell the world we're here
but the world we looked for wasn't there
so we took out a joint mortgage
on another planet, of lengthening shadows
by day, cosy silences by night;
All earthy modernity taken fright
of two very ordinary people
whose clothes, hair, ears, eyes
would have taken no one by surprise
but, rather, we'd have liked to hear it said
by more faces in glad places
while there was still time

See those two? They're friends of mine

We tried to pretend it didn't matter
because we had each other;
But now you're gone, dear friend;
I stand alone against a tide
of bitter sympathy that threatens,
just as it always did, you and I,
for all that we were two
very ordinary people, braving
the same mud, sky, as any other
pair in love - so twists of wire
that heap our grave
conspire to show

See him? His friend was gay, you know

CHANCE MEETING

In a smoky gloom I watched you standing there
Running cruisy fingers through hair
Alight with whimsy sunshine
Flickering through shutters
Set to glower the world outside,
Nursing us on the inside to a comfortable
Anonymity; and you glanced at me
Then flung your eyes back
Into a pool of drowning men
Shrieking silently for rescue
In spite of dog-paddle gestures
Defying their distress, like
The rhythm of a hit pop song
Repudiating our loneliness

Gathering up a casual air, I spoke with you,
Let the lilt of your voice wash over me
Like a friendly shower after a bad dream
And we talked in easy comradeship
While loud music screened all ghosts
From us, inciting a temporary
Deliverance; and we went outside
Into a gentler conspiracy of noon sounds
Urging us to hurry, hurry
To a kinder place - where these hands
May freely frame your face,
These lips descending, your body
Answer mine, all threat receding,
Our world turned inside out

WASTELAND 2000

Cold, crawling to the fire,
calling to none along the stony way
(Time enough to talk
once learned to walk). On, on,
pinpricks of illumination
taking captive our imagination, and
there are pumpkins;
Close, at the edge of a civilization
busy casting shadows;
(Phantoms creeping at the wall, like
aliens weeping for us all);
Modern history, taunted with chaos;
Ancients, haunting Parnassus
and no easy answers. Crawl, Tiresias!
Such is the way of humanity,
to deal the world's worst hypotheses
a crisis of sexuality
what and where (and whom) it will

Call it, political

AUGUST AND GENET

Bright eyes follow
black waves, of
handsome hair

Sweaty hands delight
in outrageous denial

Ah, beauty rare, beauty dear,
shines there, shines
here – like torchlight
on a thief

A pain grips troubled loins
makes breathing hard

Black waves
will smother a man
if he lets 'em

SEX, LIES AND STEREOTYPE

Billy was a shy boy
who came from our town,
did well at school,
never played the fool,
preferred to be alone,
had a voice as thick as honey,
kept his head in a book;
The day he said 'hello'
I didn't quite know
where to look

One day, early, I went fishing
at my favourite place;
Billy was already there,
tongues of red hair licking
at my face as I told him
to go, the sacrilege all his!
But he stood his ground
so I flung him down, a heat
in us risen - like
the dawn

Our lips brushed as if meant
and his sweet body sighed;
mine paused, replied
until spent - then
lingerings in the lap
of a songbird, no
willows weeping
or fish biting
nor word of
dissent

Down at the Angel
one evening,
drinking with the lads,
poised to win at darts,
my girl cheering…
Enter Billy with a mate
and I score a bull!
The crowd roaring,
my girl adoring,
me, hurting

like hell

SAUNA

In a heat the other day
I watched two feet
begin a play with
each other; I let you
smother my applause
and gave my body yours
nor was there time
(God only knows!)
to allow your toes, or
mine, a little bow
at the end of life's
pantomime - and Someone
to meet…

Wouldn't know the face, love
but won't forget the feet!

ON HAMPSTEAD HEATH

Copper brightly, shades of green,
pink blossom,
home kites
flying

Kaleidoscope

A groan from troubled
Lebanon, dust of Eritrea
turning the pages
of my book

Stance, a searching look

And we'll dance with the trees
in a leafy heaven, chance
how the story
ends

Briefly, friends

WELL OF LONELINESS

There's a pool
at the bottom of my mind
and sometimes
I bathe there naked,
feel free
to think about ME;
Pride sheds its pain,
sweet vanity comes
again, again!
I'll shout, float, play
(no one about
to call me out
or charge me
with indecency)
Ecstasy, Monet's
water lilies

Silicon fins
for company

Virtual reality

A MORAL TALE

I am what I am and all that I am
is the sum of my love for you

It grieved me that when we meet
I should not hug and kiss you
in the street, like that girl over there
with the bright orange hair
and her fella with the pin
in his nose, for everyone knows
the young must have their day
but it's something else
to be gay

I am what I am and all that I am
is the sum of my love for you

I went to court and made my stand
for showing the world how I feel
but the same magistrate
who put a thief on probation
took exception, chose
to pontificate on morals today
and fined me a month's pay
though not just (of course)
'cause I'm gay

I am what I am and all that I am
is the sum of my love for you

I went to work and colleagues
shook my hand, said it's good to
stand up and be counted - then
all sorts of whisperings began
and I would not resign
as tension in the office mounted,
people changing sides
every day, for what price
lunch with a gay?

I am what I am and all that I am
is the sum of my love for you

A local rag printed us, even
made us out to be the good guys
but it came as no surprise, the letters
unsigned, anonymous phone calls
designed to humiliate, dismay,
for lowering the tone, and
letting the neighbours down;
worse, preferring to go
our own way

They had the last laugh,
I keep your photograph

A PERCEPTION OF PINKS

Boy in the garden
on a white horse - saves
a fair maiden, lets legend
take its course;
Youth in the garden
declines to play - spurns
a fair maiden, lets gossip
have its way

Man in the garden
close to the earth - looking
to heaven, for its
rebirth;
The world's capacity
for pain - glimpsed
in drops of acid
rain

Come, ride a white horse
across the sky. Higher, higher!
Chance a fair maiden
and dragon's fire;
Below, pinks in the garden
in full flower. In heaven,
legends of our own
making

WISH YOU WERE HERE

Side by side, we met the tide
and plunged into the sea,
swam with the fishes - then
rose again, my love
and me

Hand in hand, we crossed the sand
smiling at everyone;
Nudge-nudge, wink-wink
on our backs, hotter
than the sun

We stayed just long enough
to gather up our stuff
and stroll the gamut, pausing
for a kiss - to oblige
the local press

We hit page three, my love
and me. Breakfast was strained
at the B&B - till one guest said
a fine pair we made, and
the rest cheered!

Over greasy eggs and bacon
and mugs of stewed tea, we
grinned happily - enjoying
a grand vacation, my gay
love and me

OSCARS

When I am with a woman
I think of her alone, no thoughts
of men as we make love
with a sure passion;
Whenever we walk, talk,
laugh, play, I would not wish
myself elsewhere - or
some man here

It doesn't work that way

The love of a good woman
(at a price above rubies),
a treasure I respect, nor
would abuse;
So why this naked pleasure
with a man, worth more
to me than rubies
do I choose?

Who knows?

LINES ON A FRIEND

He had wet dreams, a friend of mine,
fine hopes, filial ambition made sprung
from a well-ordered hearth
tossed aside as he grew bolder,
refuting homespun ideals
for a measure of global concern;
Marches here and there...
Crusades for this and that, always
hip flask and a home-made smoke
letting fly raw love in all our faces,
mindful of bony fingers pawing
at pa's snoozy chair, the
TV's plaintive glare;
Ah, but he endured a morbid
self-consciousness, this native son
of our Jerusalem!
He hit a bad patch, my friend;
empty days, heart sick of
senseless deprivation, barter
of politic passion;
No job, wore the pink with pride.
A few friends persevered;
None spoke up for him in court
save one shy parent and a sad Head
of the old school. He wept, they wept,
we wept. How it buzzed, that room,
such righteousness, suffering us
a lifetime of self-witness;
Called to account, all labour pains.

No spot on New at Ten of course
among Sinn Fein or the Princess of Wales
(just a local spread about potential
gone to seed, protesting
Gay Rights indeed!)
So to parent-child, more pain.
In pub and supermarket
love on the line, take it
or leave it

I & I

Don't wax lyrical about loneliness
                      says the Man
tell'em just what it can do,
              how it will
kill the eye, give the lie
to that so-smooth brow
              you're
scrubbing at;

Don't make out
           it doesn't pain you
to prepare for another day
                no different
from yesterday, unless
that face you're
          making
cracks!

Okay, run a comb through your hair
                      says the Man
straighten your tie
          just so;
here's your jacket,
perhaps we'll
          make it;
Come, come!

No, don't throw it
           at the cat
or rip your throat
           like that,
you'll tear my shirt;
See, now we'll be

              late
for work!

Don't swear at me
              says the Man,
it's not my fault
            you can't
stand the closet
any more. Get off
              that floor.
Now!

And blow your nose, you're
getting on my nerves

A CLOSE SHAVE

I peer into my mirror and see your eyes
smiling, your hair sleek and shining, like
a Persian preened for comment;
The mouth is smiling too – like a wine stain
on pages of a favourite book;
Look! I breathe on the glass, cannot easily
erase your worst fears in me;
Like the Cheshire Cat's, queer eyes
tease mercilessly;
I squint in a haze, blood from
a graze splashing me;
Ah, Serendipity!
Our tragedy, a predilection
for pulp fiction

RENT

Slump-shouldered denim at a crowded bar,
glancing round from time to time,
a smokescreen sneer in sloth eyes,
the better part of him at some other place
toning up the muscles in his face, like
torchlight begging a friendly spot
in some God-awful squat on a wet night,
skint. I smile and he smiles back
with tight mouth, critical eye;
I shrug them off, flirting with fancy
in my mind and, yes, I recognize the kind
just as he sees in me a lonely, balding geezer
with a good few quid to spare
for day-returns to Babylon.
He swings a hip, tongues a lip,
lets an expert hand brush his crotch,
gathering up decision from a cheap watch
while a flame in my soul, meant to keep
cheap thrills away, is fading fast;
Time, all-slowing for this phantom
of my past to catch up with me at last;
Now together, pressing knee to knee

I wonder why, why me, and whether
I have enough money?

BOLD ITALICS

Tie me up and gag me,
the strength of your personality
dominating,
the splendour of your body
subjugating,
the heat of our passion
titillating;
A common vulnerability, picture
of base humility sending
shivers down the spine
that *thrill* me

O, ecstasy!

Let hands, mouth,
tongue - *spill* me
into craven
oblivion

Captives, of our heat.
Desire, well met.

FLY AWAY, PETER

*As the shadow on the rock moves
so would I*

It's early yet and the tide's not high, so
I'll linger here among the gulling chatter
and it won't really matter

*As the shadow on the rock moves
so would I*

Summer heat's a cage, some thrice
honking horn at a page of my book
turning me

*As the shadow on the rock moves
so would I*

Grabbing at briefs (where my shoes were)
under a cackle of wings, in a globe
that's moved over

*As the shadows on the rock fly
so, so would I*

Gone now, who horned me
as waters of the earth that joined me
re-enter at a hung lip

*No shadow on the rock now
No, nor I*

A table spread before me, where I sip
wine alone and wonder how on earth
you'll manage to keep the car on

No, no shadows on the rock now
for us

You're growing old with someone else
to share - and I at least know
where my shoes are

FAMILY VALUES

A child, made to sit on your knee
and learn to tell the hour
before I was four – I hated you
for that; Coronation Day,
peering at a tiny screen,
I began to fidget (bored with
black and white pageantry)
so you got even with me;
O, thunderous rumblings!
A deafness hard to bear,
(God moving his furniture
to suit my father);
Mother, nailed to the family tree.
Brother, invariably seen and
heard on cue. No hue and cry,
but a penchant for pulp fiction
(the Smiths swanning along
nicely, thank you).
I gave what love I knew
(Precious little down to you,
none, once ma gone);
A cross to bear and can,
for no longer on the run
and hear thunder less
each time I kiss
another man

DOROTHY WHO?

Natives on my patch! Dancing, yelling,
making music; our naked joy on show,
celebrating Dorothy's rainbow as released
on video (stocked by the manager of a store
shopped for putting bias before profit);
Jury's in chaos and the Sinod;
God's keeping an open mind, rather than
be unkind to those who take bread and wine
when they can; a hard decision, given
that gays are even on television nowadays
(ratings unaffected, can you believe?);
Only to be expected, some will say
in a world where men dye their hair
and wear body spray

Must be seen to pull out all the stops
else Equal Ops caught napping
on the front benches

EBB TIDE

Black waves sucking the feet,
tugging the soul;
Distant lights pricking
the flesh, like pins
in this doll man
of yours

Ours once, a night like this!
Sea breeze, salty and sensual
like a first kiss before
passion takes over - and
sweet dreams run
for cover

We surfed the clouds,
played in craters of the moon
like children knowing
that soon - too soon,
Someone would
call us home

Black waves sucking the feet,
tugging the soul;
Sea breeze, same promises
stripping us bare;
A lifetime to share, already
gone

You, in another man's heaven.
Me, on the mudbanks of Eden.

SPRING, AUTUMN, LEICESTER SQUARE

The collar of the shirt is grubby,
patches on the jeans, torn;
Trainers on the feet,
are tied with string;
Uncombed hair, a yellowy
grey - like a watery sun
on St Swithin's Day

The eyes are older, much older
than the grin ripening all flesh
pinkly for a moment or two,
busy coining faces - drops
loosely, like a faulty bolt
on a stable door asking
for trouble

Hands mime to busker songs,
a few rights, a few wrongs,
conscious enough of a second
glance to take the wink;
So grubby collar and rolled
umbrella - head
for Eros

CHAT ROOM AGENDA

Quiet1ad and SportyOne
in cyberspace, having fun - with
aspects of character rarely shown,
shades of personality usually reserved
for the safety of isolation, or
ecstasy of masturbation;
Poet, shackled by an inferiority
complex; soccer fanatic, wishing
he had a way with syntax;
Free spirit, stuck on the inside
looking out; extrovert, needs a macho
tag like rips in a Sainsbury's bag;
Bottom goes top, king of the road;
Star performer, enjoying the ride;
Buddies, surfing fantasy
on the Internet

Could be you, me, a face in the street - or
that trolley rage git in the supermarket

BETWEEN THE ACTS

One drink to get through the night;
Another one, two, three for the road;
Animations all around look as though
they might lend an ear, a voice even
to kill this silence in the head
(requiem for an also-ran). Time, soon.
And still a waxwork on show with
nobody passing comment so might as well
Get another one in and just
GO

Over there, someone I used to know.
Can't hurt to say 'hello' surely?
Eyes flash, 'No way, dearie!'
One step forward, freeze, back on the rack
like a see-through plastic mac.
Boozing again, praying for rain.
Nearly ready to quit this place,
settle for a haunting of care-lines
in the face, gold in the hair.
Gotta have one more beer

Fool's gold? We'll never know, you and I,
strangers till we die, wondering where
love has gone, why no one wants to know
the secrets of a heart so full it's overflowing
with pity - and making a mess;
Fat chance of happiness! And why should you
help clean up my distress? How dare I
paw your privacy like some home seeking
stray cat? Small wonder you keep
well away from that …

Life's a bitch! I clutch the glass,
drawn a short straw, left to drown
in my jealousy. Why me? Dare I
chance speaking? Needs must, I suppose.
Beats sneaking home, tail between legs
as usual. Besides, who knows?
We might dance, chat, or better still,
get out of here (your place or mine?),
take a trip to see that ole Wizard of Oz.
Because, because, because

I catch a smouldering glance, throw a grin;
Mouth tightens, gold turns to lead again.
A hand gropes mine. I swing round and see
brave eyes inviting, lips parted hopefully.
I grimace (wrong time, wrong place). I scowl
and move on, glimpse a wolf on the prowl
seize my Golden One. They leave together
for a fun-night stand. How I know that look!
I've sung the song, read the book, seen
the show. *Sugar.* Time to go.

FAMILY TIES

O, how I long to be free!
In a world usurping Nature's crown
of maternal anxiety

And I would assuage paternity
though not for me, ambition's clown.
O, how I long to be free!

I seek good company
to lift the heart, ease the frown
of maternal anxiety.

A gay inspiration fills me
(or in paternal conflict, surely drown);
O, how I long to be free!

Father, will you walk with me?
Our jealousy put down,
of maternal anxiety...

What matter, the stains of history
on a cherished christening gown?
O, how I long to be free
of maternal anxiety!

BETWEEN FRIENDS

Under a halo of sudden light
a familiar figure beckons;
Looks, sure to win the devil over;
Designer gear, angels would
give their wings for;
Laugher lines in the classic brow,
enigmatic poise, teasing
me - even now!
Into the clinging dew, I'll run barefoot,
hug anew this pouting saint
to a sobbing breast;
Laughter, through tears!
For all these years, parted
broken-hearted;
Catching my breath, no nearer it seems
to this golden haired god in jeans
I've borrowed before;
Reaches out a hand, indulging me
a smile that means so much,
I'd give my *all* to touch;
Like a lark into dawn skies, vanished!
A bitter-sweet song, no listener
left unpunished

Our lives, as fresh as spring rain
till you tried heroin

BLUE EYES

He sat at a table by the window
staring into space, eyes like dewdrops
on a bluebell among shadows
haunting the handsome face
like city kids playing
among the last flowers
of spring

I lost myself in those eyes,
wandered territory unknown without fear,
guided by the sad sunshine of a smile
along trails I'd never dare for their twists
and turns - Nature run wild, its call
like the heartbeat
of a wilful child

We found each other and he took
my hand, gently pulled me to the ground;
Our first kiss was like coming home
after long years away - and
he made love to me there;
O, the beauty, ecstasy,
cruelty of despair!

Suddenly, he got up and went out in the rain.
I finished my drink and went home alone.

AWAKENINGS

Lying in your bed
in the middle of the night,
I nibble your ear - and
give you a fright!

Riding a storm,
I ease your shorts down;
My tongue in your cheek
pleads penetration

As your body responds
to my sensuous heat,
we take a decision
not to retreat

Wave after wave
to a safe shore we tumble
each other, drenching the sheets
with intimate laughter

Becalmed at last,
we Creatures of the Deep
turn over - and go
back to sleep

THE QUILT MAKERS' SONG

Life! Let me not hunger
for all I cannot be, but
suffer me a passion for
what's gone before;
Let me build cathedrals,
flare them high, dedicated
to my better selves
so they may rest easy
in a shade, against crosses
made by matchstick men,
losses we shall count again
when the time comes
to account for more
than dreams. *Life, not*
all it seems

Love! Let me not beg
at the roadside, but
give freely and let's
paint pictures to last
centuries, windows
stained with all the colours
of our lovemaking;
Let those who come after us
be together in their turn
and lift an eye for knowing
this; and we shall share
each kiss again, again
again – we matchstick
men. *Love, not*
all our pain

Death! Let me not weep
for those I have loved;
Let there be candles lit
in each airy cathedral,
saintly with sunshine,
ringing out with rain, our
seasons come again!
Smiles of joy among the tears
to mark this, the salvation
of our fears, a passing
through chance memories,
celebration of our years;
butterfly wings across
a garden. *Dead, and
who's forgiven?*

WHO DARES, WINS

Love is all - to live and die for, yet
some would say, often bitterly,
one kind better to ignore, forget,
even in the 21st century

Our love took root, grew tall and fair
in a shady corner of Eden;
Many who looked and saw it there
begged a cutting for their own garden

Most folk simply walked straight past,
believing it best for everyone;
Others took sticks and stones to cast,
any excuse better than none

In the sun! Behold gay love, its beauty…
though none so blind that will not see

GAY PRIDE

When I wake, your face
like sunshine in my eyes,
your breath like turning leaves
in a misty autumn rain,
I fall in love again, again!
Lips, like rose petals
parted to receive dawn's
first light, my life's
fuller frame though angels
call us names as we kiss
and hearts miss a beat

at heaven's gate

HIDDEN AGENDA

Pulling this way and that
Like some tug-of-war rope
Across a stream;
Mixed feelings, striving
For supremacy over
A bad dream;
Patterns of illusion, conspiring
Against a nether reality – for
Its very spirituality;
Soul in confusion, aspiring
To the freedom - of
A native identity

Gender and sexuality versus
Stereotype society

Part V

LOVE AND HUMAN REMAINS

AFFAIRS OF THE HEART

No grief
finer than a kiss, inflicting
mortality on this body
barely spent with our
lovemaking, caressing
lips with secret smile, seeking
the Creator, Destroyer
in us all with Delilah's
gall – and Samson
a star pupil

No madness
in the weirdest shadows
flirting with twilight,
teasing the sun's embers
with a scattering of stars
brighter by far than the eyes
haunting this mortal frame;
Only sadness for a leaf,
fallen at our feet
before its time

No tears
(a misty rain in the wind)
nor cries from the heart
but a nightingale for others
of our kind, covering us
like a death sheet as a mark
of respect for this baring
of such reckoning as
Cassiopeia sharing
out gifts

TO AN EXPRESS, ON TIME running

Between lilac sheets we lay,
taking on the world,
its Word sure
to win

Harder, harder fires the dawn,
scorching all leafy flesh
that ever clung, sung

Now, a shrill siren
drenches us;
Myriad voices
frighten

At the smouldering ruin
of your face, the 6.15
dumps me

Guard, blow your worst
over us;
A godly sinning
covers us

TIME WARP

Yesterday, a stranger
in the Square
asked the way
to heaven-knows-where
but I could not reply
for a shade of hair
and manner of walk
(bright eyes, curve of lip,
small talk)
lit up a shadowy
corner of the heart;
Memories, thought well hid
in a closet - where
dreams we shared still hang
like old favourites
gone out of fashion, ghosts
of our passion

SUNSET ON A COUNTRY CHURCHYARD

A subtle blush haunts the sky,
makes glow anew the haggard visage
of a long day's dying;
Owl, flying the killing fields;
Confetti, where hearses passed
for wedding cars (answer to
a mother's prayers);
A clapping like bats' wings
for fraternity's sake
in the womb-tomb of our history
at this, my wake;
Fireflies, obscuring photographs
of us like smoke

The moon's up. A rabbit darts
for cover. Owl knows
better. How soon
it's all over!

BLUEPRINT FOR A ONE-NIGHT STAND

Slowly descending ceiling stills,
squat walls settle;
All the colours of night-clamour
dissemble into a stale dawn
glimpsed through ragged curtains
at a wry window

Mind, stretching;
Body, smoothing over its cracks
in foetus cradle, summoning succour
from a worldly benevolence
stinging sweetly at some
leafy breast.

Tears, oozing from a breathless
dreaming on this, the marble slab
of rude awakening - dispel
a fleeting trust that today
might return us cosy
kitchen sounds.

Together, we lit a candle
in the darkness of our nigh;
How it flared, a heavenly light!
Alas, I fear, better to leave you
sleeping here – than chance
discovering who we are
who we are?

SALUTE TO A PROSTITUTE

practised hands shape
this slave flesh

subtle hands serve
a brave desire

urgent hands shift
a murmuring grief

all-knowing hands paw
a forsaken immunity

                                warm hands
                                bluff me

                                token hands
                                move me

                                hot fingers
                                goading

                                all my senses
                                urging me

                                out of myself, oh
                                so briefly!

STRANGERS ON A TRAIN

Met someone on a train
(was it yesterday?)
heading away from things
held dear, meant little any more
after Fate knocked on my door
smelling of adventure
(a heady perfume)
and like a fool
I let you in;
Must have been
a devil on my shoulder
getting bolder
as I get older, feel a need
to show the world
I'm not afraid
or, to tell the truth
(as told on the train)
lonely for my Youth
again, again!
So we danced all night
and the devil sang;
(To hell with what's
right and wrong!);
One life, let's have fun,
where's the harm? None,
thought I. But one by one
the flowers in my garden
began to die, till a day came
when you looked, frowned
and said goodbye

Couldn't face friends then
so caught the first train;
A stranger looked me in the eye,
said not to cry but learn
to live with pain
and love again

So I did, just as that face
in the train window said

PICKING UP THE TAB

Darker than darkness, this
dreaming of you;
Harsher than a gull's cry,
the silence;
Treading, a swell of despair
and it's a rare angel who'll
care much (if at all)
for the poor fool
sleeping off a hangover
of lovemaking bargained
for with ecstasy and paid
for - oh, so dearly!
Fine feathers, smashed
in glorious flight;
Dawn memories, splashed
with whose guilt?

OUT OF SEASON

We have romped
secret fields
a friend, and I
made pretty music
on a tin whistle
watched leaves fly
tongued by smoky grass
sung by airy choirs!
Now I alone
among wedding guests
shall sip no wine
at toasts

already, ghosts

NIGHT MOVES

in your sleep
        a finger revels
in bareness
        against your silk;
my finger reaches for it,
        your silk shifts away;
at dead of night
        two fingers mime
our lives'
        farce

SINGLES

Wake up to a buzzing
of traffic on the M-way;
Crickets in a cornfield
don't stand a chance;
Days ahead, scratching
at a bald patch;
Frantic creases
on the sheet, tracking
money spiders
at a Dance of Death;
No imprint of your feet
heating the cold spots
in our bed; no clean shirt,
odd socks across the floor;
In a too-big wardrobe,
the clothes you used to wear
leap out at me
like shadows in a mist
(hands at my throat);
Threat of no-heaven, strangling
like a farewell kiss;
(Worlds away, words to say);
Bad day done, run down
by trolleys in the supermarket
(one basket, fair game);
Tentacles, dragging your name
into nether regions
crying out for another beer
(gotta grin and bear it);
Running for cover in sweat bars
where singles gather
like predators, stalking
our dreams

Pretend lovers, in a heat over
flavoured condoms

LOVE LETTERS IN AN ATTIC

Wings of a dove
across centuries
of pain, love;
(Tears shed, taken
as read);
So glides our history
Time's passage;
Life's sadness forsworn,
a madness forgiven;
Caress me, thrill me,
enduring bird,
each faded quill
a tender word;
Laughter, a symphony
inspiring me,
its echoes cheering,
we lovers pairing;
Twin doves winging
Time's corridor,
deserving more
than acid rain

Outside world
ever learn?

THE LAST KISS

Take hold of me now!
I'll not cry out, or drop a tear
for what might come
from lips (once loud)
like the sun's fast-gathering
shroud over this head
laid here, where
you are

Let worlds collide, the
heat of our curiosity
keeps us alive

LOVE AFTER DEATH

Pick a star shining brightly,
Let it light your darkness nightly,
Find peace

A goodnight kiss

As the sun resumes its place
In our heavens above,
Enjoy, embrace

Eternal love

LOOKS FAMILIAR

Lying in the grass,
studying the sky
as cloud faces drift by
like the years of my life
from cradle to now,
wondering where have they
gone and why, where, how?
Grandad and grandma,
long since in the urn;
Family and friends
I have loved and those
who gave love in return;
Teachers, liked and loathed
who rarely understood
how hard some kids
find it to be good at this
or that, so get tagged
for trouble at an early age
and few bother to turn
the next page in their history
so – misery! Prison faces
putting on a show, or they know
they are done for; all of us
puppets on invisible strings,
praying for better things
but to what or whom? Faces
in a global room looking out,
too scared to shout for Love
and Peace or even kindness
as Apollo and lesser gods
make sport with us

IN REMEMBRANCE OF TIMES PAST

Table spread with photographs,
your scarf on my chair, beer
cans everywhere;
Thoughts of you, squabbling
over scraps, like birds on
the window sill;
Dignity - like an old cat
glimpsed in shadow,
plump and still;
Out of sheer frustration,
will dive for
a thrush

Diary of a lush

LOVE AND HUMAN REMAINS

United, we stood tall
among small folk;
When we spoke our vows
they cheered and we heard
angels in the wind,
blessings of a kind
we never knew as two people
living separate lives,
dreaming colours white
each lonely night, loving
and dreading that first
kiss of sunlight
on a wet pillow

Divided, brow to brow
among small folk,
vows no easier put aside
that grown old and apart,
watched sadly by friends
and family, champions
of the heart's cause, who
cheered at high hopes
riding white horses
into love truth, glory,
while angels told stories
about Adam, Eve
and poor Judas

HOME ALONE

Half-listening to the stereo, as anxious voices
overhead prick a lampshade by our bed,
sounding out those undead I've lost
for putting a career first;
Raise a glass to every singer, every song;
Each creak, groan and frantic moan
reminding how wrong, so wrong
to live alone;
Over a frothy rim, tell the moon (peeping
behind curtains carelessly drawn) how
we planned this very room, you and I;
Seems only yesterday

All quiet now above. Empty, the hourglass
you bought me one Christmas

Nothing lasts, but love
and loneliness

IF ONLY

I wouldn't leave
the safety of my job,
the comfort of my town,
so you went alone

I waved you off
on a fast train, thinking
I would see you again
before long

I was wrong, but
still tell 'em it's alright
down the Angel
every night

I wouldn't leave
the safety of my job,
the comfort of my town
so you went alone

If only I'd known

A HISTORY OF ABUSE

Under a rainbow digging for gold
until the sun goes in and my blood
runs cold at the first hint of intrusion
into my dreams, world split
at the seams!
Confusion, a worse pain than dying
of fright, but can't run away
(where to go?) or cry aloud even,
gagged and trussed by the same
shroud sheet you tucked me up in
last night, long ago;
Now, the sun again! Skin gone cold
among the ruins of a day grown old
before its time;
(No tears for dead nursery rhyme
or gold to ransom
lost children)

Asleep, tossed on horns.
Awake, a print of hooves
forever to remain, like
fractured lifelines
in acid rain

THE EMPTY NEST

Swallows flown to better climes,
sounds of half-forgotten summers
tucked in forked
feathers

Bailiffs, beating
at the door

HALFWAY HOUSE

Born in an empty house,
number seven on the door;
Left crying in a towel
at someone else's door;
Had a few good homes
and a good few schools
but never quite learned
the house rules, or earned
a place in anyone's heart,
branded a hopeless case
from the start;
Ended up in a squat,
getting by on the street,
selling sex at the going rate;
Punters come and go,
(some friends even)
but none stay long,
at number seven

ALL DRESSED UP AND NOWHERE TO GO

Tables in a room
at Happy Hour;
forced laughter
booming like canon
across no man's land!
Lots of food and drink
so let's not think
about tomorrow, or mind
tears in the wind;
Give us a tune on the keys
and we'll sing along
to the accordion man
(who'll cheer us up if anyone can)
while the old gods tease
among themselves
about the rights and wrongs
of strings we pull
at each other
across the floor;
A banging at the door
(let 'em in, the more
the merrier!)
No one scrapes a chair
(nobody hears)
like toys seen better days
discarded by peers
grown out of their inhibitions
and found better ways
to spend an evening
than a gathering
of fictions

BUS STOP

Time passes
like a double-decker bus
rumbling down the High Street
looking for the likes of us
to stick out a hand
and make it stop, the way it did
in pouring rain that day
we jostled in a queue
for a 29 (running late
as usual) anxious to be home;
We began to chat
about this 'n that, though
I didn't quite catch
everything, your sweet smile
winging me a tenderness
long forgotten (on my own, last
love flown!) Now, I'll not stay
my heart's leaping
for keeping you company
at bars, clubs, cinemas
to ease our soul its pain
and rediscover in each other
an alternative freedom

CHARYBDIS MON AMOUR

Whirlpool

Anguish, mirrored
in eddies of shrapnel light;
Pain, caught fast
in a grip of mute supplication;
Loneliness, laid bare
in a mad rape

*Round, round, this raving soul
chases its own dear folly*

Life, long since perjured
for roller coaster thrills;
Love, all scratched
and bleeding after spills,
spreadeagled
on a cross

Lord, have mercy on us

No screaming brakes
at Salvation's door
left ajar;
Nor one kind echo
in the blind
drop

A CLASS ACT

Come early, love

Under the crabby stair
let's bundle
all the time we have
before that first fierce tread
shakes down, on
your fine head - hints
at other things

And you'll leave me quickly
to tidy the fraying cuff
that ticks me

CLOSE FRIENDS, DISTANT LIVES

I see the moon, you see the sun;
another time, another place;
On the ground, perceive a snail
trying to keep pace with it all.
Our faces lit, now dark,
laughing, weeping, waking, sleeping;
World, turning on a snail.
I see the sun, you see the moon;
same day, same night;
In our hearts, a secret place
where old friends meet
to laugh, talk and play
until our time is up, for
even snails sleep.
I close my eyes and see you,
feel your heart beating
under my shirt, your breath
on my face; as good at time
as any to embrace
our history - against which
all else pales

Such is the significance
of snails

DANCE WITH A STRANGER

Seasons come and go, every one
different, like old faces that help
make our lives complete;
To each, a memory bitter-sweet
like familiar places that help
make our lives complete;
Photograph and frame, you and I;
Seasons, memories, linger on
like a favourite dance score;
Own room, a virtual dance floor.
Your face, I adore - and whore
the voice with a punter's passion,
every second with you feeding
obsession, though each heartbeat
conceding a lost cause

Radio days

DIRECTOR'S CUT

A heat's on, dripping
from the screen;
Sweet seduction, as celluloid
carnality slips into sub-reality
under the skin of what passes
for conventional identity;
Good to relate to movie beat!
Brushing a stranger's thighs
in a hard seat, weaving
dangerous lies, in
a cold sweat;
Movie lovers doing okay,
their wonders to perform,
an overt sexuality
turning blue buffs on
before and after the lights
go down;
Day returns to Babylon
outside office hours;
Madding crowd booking
into film theatres, alias
Smith and Jones
up for the best lines,
a leading role, directing
the action - soul for soul;
Close shot: penetration, ecstasy,
Love's rolling stone;
Beautiful people, amen.
Small sacrifice, a stain
on integrity's underwear
(will clean)

Cinema's jest, illusion.

FRIENDS

I did a friend a favour
though it put me
on the rack

I asked the friend
a favour and he
turned his back

Hail-fellow-well-met
on a one-way
street

MATINS

As dawn's first light bathes the head
in sweeter dreams than dead of night,
so tread my loves in nether realms
of consciousness. Rumbling storm,
a graver sorrow to the Sandman
than long-since haunts plagued
even now by taunts of bogie men
dragging us down. Apollo, moving on
as I cannot - for thunder in the ears
dare I forget

Roll back the years, but still no rest!
And will angels dry our tears
before breakfast (in time
to make the best of things),
the day run true to form,
cock robin at the heart of things,
a corpse still warm? Inspiration,
sounds of celebration
for what was, is and
yet shall be

Ah, sweet mystery!

THE LOVERS

Scarce we talked of love
Scarce we talked at all

I would scan the paper
While you got the tea
Or prune my roses
While you watched me
Out of the corner of one eye
At your herbaceous border
Busy with a trowel

Scarce we talked of love
Scarce we talked at all

I would fix whatever
While you made us a cuppa
And when I'd finished
We would sip comfortably
In our favourite places
Glancing up now and then to
Read each other's faces

Scarce we talked of love
Scarce we talked at all

Now I prattle away
In a misty rain
Bring you roses where you lie
In a patch of cemetery
Birds for company
Wondering why, oh why?
Again and again

Scarce we talked of love
Scarce we talked at all

LEGEND

Clear sky, no breeze in the hair,
heart light because you're here
in this leafy vault where all life
endures and bluebells ring changes
no one hears. We came, saw everything,
caught the first cuckoo of spring,
did right by a fox left rotting,
regret nothing. But a wind's up 'n cold
for an earthworm's pace at this
favourite place. Time to run, our
epitaph for anyone to see

Two hearts on a tree

MATES

Sharing bread with seagulls
that dive a rolling foam,
you worked a passage home
to this uninspiring shore
where a rebel heart demanded more
than nine-to-five sweat propping
up the bar on a Saturday night
so packed a bag and sailed away
to warmer climes, better times;
Sent picture postcards every day
from wild, exotic places
to old, familiar faces getting by
on a cheese 'n pickle,
where home thoughts
are apt to fly

Full circle

DAYDREAM BELIEVER

Days in, days out, touting for friends;
Love, by any other name.
No tears on the face of a clown
at first sight - or hint of stains
on a pillow every night.
Fairy tales told around a DJ's
talent for importuning on local radio;
Dream ticket for karaoke at singles night,
everyone keen to get it right
(a packet in every pocket);
Grape pickers treading barefoot
over best laid plans, wine stains
on the cover of *Radio Times*

THE LONGEST JOURNEY

Love has many faces,
some gay, some not,
journeys many places,
laughs, cries a lot…
No finer friend you'll find
to share peace of mind
whenever demons on the brain
come again, again
for the soul
or we fall

Love has many faces,
comforts, make afraid
in least expected places,
reflecting all that's made us
tearful, sublime,
captives of Time;
In a world not of our choice
its sweeter voices
ease the soul
or we fall

Love has many reasons,
asks questions, tells lies;
a face for all seasons
where need flies…
In the heat of human sorrows,
through crumbling tomorrows;
Brave hearts on wing
in spite of everything
that drags on the soul
or we fall

My love, it wears a friend's face,
makes no demands;
A single candle placed
at your heart's command…
Under threat of darker sorrows,
striving better tomorrows;
A light in the soul's gloaming
to guide an epic roaming
at freedom's call
or we fail

Part VI

TRIUMPH OF THE SPIRIT

MILLENNIUM DAWN

Will it rise like an angel
with wings of gold,
compounding all the tales
told - about a new Eden?
A sign perhaps, reward
even? For the better
achievements of Man
than acid rain;
Or will it flicker drab
and grey like a dress
shop window, on
St Swithin's Day?
Shall we take hope from
valiant hues, or mope
for a tell-tale heart's
home truths?

Whatever pain, whatever
glory - in each weird
and wonderful dawn
the story of Man

Read on

WATERS OF THE WOMB

Sea of faces gathered round,
offering a helping hand
where I cower in my corner
from wind and acid rain
eroding a world whimpering
in pain

Waiting to die

Sea of hands reaching out
to drag me to my feet,
let me stand tall among
small folk (rat race run
to win), wise men
looking on

In vain

Waves of well-meaning thought
wash over me, less support
than surfing in a storm
towards a blind shore, our
memories no more than
a fistful of straws

Telling lies

So, close these eyes with all
the delicacy of mortal sweat
and let me go among others
drowning too, in a world where
politics and religious divide,
leave no place to hide

Or pride

Ocean of voices, defying
a crashing hypocrisy,
calling on me to ride the tide
at the Surfer's side, taking
the swell in our stride
and all for love

Let me live

THE LONGEST DAY

Knocking on doors, nobody there.
Called on the phone, no replies.
Tried the local surgery (come back
in three days) and, sorry the Samaritans
are busy; went to church in desperation,
but - closed for restoration; found
a priest for advice (a kindly man) but
if I didn't mind, he had a Bible class
at ten. Even stopped people in the street.
Did *no-one* care? And where was God?
Glanced at the sun as a huge cloud
passed over, saw people run for cover
(what's the use?). Walked on and on,
no pride or purpose; mile after mile.
Darkness couldn't come too soon.
Glanced at the moon – and something
in the Old Man's smile made me feel
less alone, lit a candle in my soul
that led me home

INTENSIVE CARE

Eerie vault, the colour of snow;
Weary mind, a yen to go sledging
on Blueberry Hill. Dark sound
tearing at the ears (might have been
laughter, but too many fears
come tumbling after). See, hear, smell.
That's all. Walls of silk, like
an open coffin. Would-be mourners,
like milk bottles on a doorstep
that someone forgot to cancel.
Kind words, a constant hum
carving me up for the family album.
Would pray, but nothing comes of trying,
only pain - and a question of dying
best left unsaid, so back to sleep instead
and chance waking up again
for a general examination of my flaws.
Angels pause to peer in my face,
bid for my soul

What *is* that smell? Sanctity or cruelty,
I know it well

TRIUMPH OF THE SPIRIT

Had a visitor yesterday, hair thin
and grey, face lined with age
as if Time had turned a page
too many, drawn almost to a close
like veins on the hands,
stains on the clothes;
A half-smile, cracked and dry
split the papyrus skin, mouldy lips
sucking in the dust of a room
starved of good company,
deserving far better
than this travesty
of humanity

Askance, I pondered the skeleton
of someone I once knew well;
Is it but Time, I asked myself,
has done this thing - or maggots
in the soul? Whatever, it won't do at all.
I argued straight, no punches pulled
as rage lit a fire in me for this
burnt-out page of history;
So time and tide won't wait on ceremony,
so what? Are we slaves to probability,
bound to be all we're not,
a stranger's empathy
our tragedy?

No loser here, in the castle of my skin
nor any mirror win

CLASSROOM POLITICS

Murmurs in the classroom
smack of revolution

Stuck in front of a television,
well able to tell fact from
fiction, problem being
where to draw the line between
what we need to see, over
endless cups of tea - and reject
whenever we suspect
our pleasure a shade
unhealthy?

Murmurs in the classroom
smack of revolution

Made to sit back and watch
our planet being set upon;
An indifference to Nature
but for a public relations
exercise - put on by fat cats
exploiting media attention,
all the better to disguise
a hidden agenda, of
mass destruction

Murmurs in the classroom
smack of revolution

Young voices raised in
anxious discussion;
Disenchanted with politics,
history and religion;
Dare argue for the future
of next generations, dispute
their elders have a head start
or leaders our best interests
at heart

*Suffer the children, hope
of a millennium*

PILGRIM

Pearly sky, inching open its portals
to all wanderers in the world, anxious branches
dripping rebirth on wintry head. All music dives
after Noah's dove. Each knee bends, for
love or hell of it. Inching forward, no time
to rest - though back be bent and heart
but lent to a photograph at the breast.
Welcome back the swallow (once envied
madly) nor think badly of human frailty
trudging unchartered grief. Pause awhile.
Glimpse a gentler smile drip pearls, on
heavier tread than ever we'd have said
or the world know for sure just how dense
a path its pilgrims thread - whose battle hymn
swings a cruel lead at worship, at war.
On, on, Myth Breaker (to Greenham - if
you must), rainbow brasses scheming
to penetrate our dreaming.

Peace on Earth, our eternal theme.
Swallow's arc conspiring with grace
to fill an empty space. (Pilgrim's desire
braving a lesser freedom in prayer).
Beware puny passions upon our dread
nor trust that else unsaid compensate
for any failure to contemplate branches
overhead - to Nature's satisfaction

Worldly congregation, straining at the bit
for a pearl at market

POSTCARDS FROM BERLIN

The wall is down!
A freedom dearly won.
Now echoes of the past
drift East, West,
spread concern among
veterans

The wall is down!
An irony of photographs
left to haunt quiet
corners East, West,
keep a vigil for
the curious

The wall is down!
Politics gone mad,
the papers say,
fighting East, West,
for the best
headlines

The wall is down!
A freedom dearly won;
Now, war's on
for the peace dividend;
East, West, world
without end

BURIED ALIVE

At tuneful mind strings
plucks a distant April night,
fills the eye with sweetest
melancholy, draws me under
the world into a fine death
where no one can enter
to make me

BODY POSITIVE

Life, death!

Floods me, goads me,
Leads me beside hot beaches
Where I run, a dazzling sea
Cheering me on, and I wonder
Where the lark has gone
That fixed me with its cheer
Before abandoning me here
Like a forgotten toy
Filled with the joy of its
Having played me out
Before going about
Nature's own
Business

Life, death!

Calls me, galls me,
Urges me back, back to you;
But we are gone, the taste of us
Honey on my tongue
Where we romped and played
Like tots in make-believe
Heading barefoot among jellyfish
For the Punch and Judy man
Who'll make us laugh
If anyone can
Before the sun goes down
And our time
Forgotten
Life, death!

Overtaken us now, beckoning;
I'll not rush my pace, for
We already ran our race, won
A place among these stars
Enchanting this lulling swell.
All's well; one lost toy recovered
And taken home, Punch and Judy
In a packing case sleeping it off
At some Bed and Breakfast;
I, filled with such a night
Far exquisite for words
Like those we shared
Before AIDS

POTTERY CLASS

so stubborn!
clinging to the sun's
Midas wheel;
brass monkeys singing
at a funeral;
so, the poet's season
teasing Time
at leafy whim; rhyme
nor reason
let shades of delusion
make love-lines
in the clay; each dusty
day, more moaning
beasts thrown to a vision
(ceramics, just
for show) in exhibition
on Death Row

RICHES IN THE CLAY

Come the world's end
some makeshift
dawn - What to do?
Where to run?
Anyone to hold
my hand, mine
theirs?

Or, left to fend alone
against the cold
in the fullness
of our years?

Who cares?

Most folk couldn't
give a damn - but
for their own
pleasure

Those who do, whatever
colour, creed, political
feed - our planet's treasure
forever to cherish,
a Testament to Love
though humanity
near perish.

A PHOENIX IN SOHO

Ordinary people passing by,
having fun in bars, folk
like you and me, no aliens from Mars
come to threaten the planet;
some sipping coffee at a roadside café
enjoying a chat, warm spring sunshine
on the face, trails of laughter
like wedding lace;
Suddenly, the sky turns black!
Smell and roar of the Devil on our back
as heaven looks away in despair
and ordinary people learn
the true meaning of fear;
Death and destruction everywhere,
wedding lace in tatters;
Ordinary people, discovering
what matters and playing their part
straight from the heart;
Smoke clears, sun reappears,
world keeps turning;
Finger of blame points, charges,
moves on;
Ordinary people, rising above tragedy
or the Devil win - pray we never
see the like again;
Small comfort for those left to writhe
in the throes of loss and pain
but hope for us all - as we learn
to live and love again, no matter
the colour of our skin
or the creed we live by
or our sexuality
Amazingly, yesterday, a complete

stranger said 'hello' over a cappuccino
in Soho; and there was wedding lace
in the street, ordinary people rising
above their tears and fears, bringing
hope and love for years to come

Or what chance, children
of the millennium?

WISHFUL THINKING

A Peace rose grows
by our gate

Folk pause at
its frothy rim
with eyes bright
like firelight
on cosy windows
in a bad
storm

Heads bowed,
hurry home

UNIVERSAL SOLDIER

Wrestling in the womb
with thoughts I cannot know,
feelings unable to show,
I start to grow...
the way of all humanity
that's gone before, a personality
and identity to call my own
though I take my place
in a world anxious for a face,
to place here, there, within
the confines of a history
classroom taught, and
purpose-built

Wrestling in the womb
with thoughts I cannot know,
feelings unable to show,
I continue to grow...
a microcosm of all human
endeavour, facing the complexities
of Fate without a murmur,
one to one with God
without fear of the world's
goading icons, relishing centuries
of silence brought soundly
to bear upon Man's first
cry – *war, war, war!*

REFUGEES

It came upon me suddenly
and seized my mind, as cruelly
as the century left behind;
Rain, tearing at my back!
A darkness in the soul;
Wind, crass and loud - like
a soccer crowd jeering
an own goal

He came upon me suddenly
and seized my hand, as boldly
as the century left behind;
Warmth, filling my heart!
A candle in the soul;
Fear, ebbing like some feisty
tide - once taken
its toll

To safety and shelter he led me,
unmasked, unmanned - like
the century left behind, its
various poses of bigotry
prejudicing history;
Old gods, wearying of the war
zone - beat a retreat, let
humanity win

21st century Man, or clones
out of Eden?

HEAVEN CAN WAIT

Local park, lonely tree,
child looks up
in a bloody pool, who
should be at school;
Tall, grown old,
branches outflung
at a brave new world;
Small and sad, kid in uniform
hugs a photograph
before taking a penknife, to
scratch out a life
on rough bark. Tree submits.
(Hanging skylark lets out a cry,
as chick-in-the-nest
prepares to fly)
Climb, climb!
Terra out of mind;
Bullies down our way, chaff
on the wind ...
Tears for mum and dad and pal
heffalump;
Gran and grandpa, show 'em all,
not afraid to jump.
A still, small voice whispers
in the ear:
Look! Beyond that runny nose
there's still a way
clear – to confide bully fear
in Someone near
and (who knows?) eventually
make it disappear

        And it did, I know. That kid
           at the Hanging Tree
      long ago, but walked away
            free – was me

BRAVEHEART

Cowering in darkest corners
of the mind - like a child
besieged by gremlins
in the dark

Captive of untried aspirations,
tugging at the chains
of well-meant
expectations

Who knows their limitations
has the strength of Samson,
locks shorn - by frustrated
ambition

Breaking free! Let those who
who know better for me
reason how - my own
person now

RESURRECTION

I drop my eyes into a flowery pool,
see the veins of one gay cheek split,
baring a thread of ash light

Against cold stone trickles
a crimson grief. On angry fingers
fall hot tears

By chance alone, a friendly breeze
has spilt this, Nature's blood; not so,
a rebel heart - tearing, crushed

Petals, like confetti on the ground;
Our bodies, whimpering without sound;
Seeds, scattered in the wind

Among the wreaths, a rose laid low
yet as I make
to go…

Risen again, newly crowned!
No glad petals to shine - but looks
familiar, embracing mine

One by one, the letters of your name
break off the stone,
prick the pool

This the moment, this the Peace;
you and I together, making ripples
forever

Amen

IN A WORD

Lord, I know not who
or what you are or where
you be, yet I feel a Presence
in the very heart of me
and Spirit as much a part
of me as the sun by day
and moon by night, shedding
heavenly light upon a world
that knows precious little
for sure, where darkness
would grip the very soul
were Someone not here,
there, everywhere - to urge
us on to better things
and better ways than else
we'd know without
a Light to show;
Lord, Word, whisperings
in the ear (and none so deaf
that will not hear) let us shed
the shackles of history
and exchange our chains
for a joining of hands
in Peace and Love
no matter colour, creed
or other division

On earth, as it is in heaven

SURFING

Surely, the tide, as surely as my life
At this place where dreams must end
And all fears come. Oh, how I wished
Things different, waters of the womb
Taken me to another place than such waves
Dragging me down! And I see your face
In a brave moon straining to catch
The dawn - as would I, or I die.
Surely, the tide, as surely as dreams
Of fame, fortune, someone to care;
When they laughed, you shrugged the score
Taking on more than I bargained for
And I wouldn't chance your blushes
But hung back, to let you ride white horses
With the pack – to hell and back!
Surely, our lives, as surely as pride
Picking at my bones. I love you!
Yet only had time for this tide's amen,
None for its daily giving and taking;
You shy like a wild thing at the world's taunts,
Refuse to be dragged into line, braving heaven
Head-on. Now! A sure tide's surfing me
Where I want to be, with you!
Who wore a sandman's mask but tore it off
To prove how some dreams last;
Soulmates, drowning in the world's nightmares
Saved! On this, our first BIG wave

Part VII

A CHRISTMAS CAROL

CHRISTMAS AT THE GOING RATE

Starling on the snowy bough,
where will you go now
as you stir your wings to fly
across this sorry sky?
Better off than I, stuck here
(sitting pretty enough in a world
dishing pity to its cardboard men);
I pause and you disappear;
Bells ring out Christmas cheer
to celebrate the Church's share
in a saviour for all seasons, who
taught the heart needs not its reasons
to care about another, rich or poor,
saint or sinner. A tramp passes.
Good souls pause to wipe their glasses
and better their chances
on Judgement Day - doling out
a sweet reprieve of misery
(and all for 50p). Now, let's hurry,
we'll be late; carols at eight
or was it nine?

Thinly drawn, cardboard line

CHASING THE DRAGON

One night in December
dragons roamed London town
in a rainy mist curtaining down
on carols in the Square;
Nine-to-five heroes making cheer,
gloamy lights in red-rim eyes
quizzing here; there, ghosts
of Christmas grabbing shelter
in a doorway, foot nudging
a cradle of rags that's stirred.
snored, slept on, not worth
a second glance; so let's lead
a merry dance through the streets,
wondering where those beasts
have gone whose scales turn brightly
in the forest nightly?

I saw no dragons, their roarings
of distress and pain blinding me
like acid rain; no end in sight
but light under a door, a whore
my saviour! Together, scared
of Christmas

ANGEL WATCH, 2000 A.D.

Through a hole in the sky,
a star wishing Christmas
on a pair roasting
chestnuts;
Kids in the street below
grab all the comfort and joy
that ever was, courtesy
of Santa's grotto;
Light, cause for celebration.
Darkness, no more than
a natural diversion
for the duration;
A minute's silent prayer, for
poor souls everywhere
running for cover
at Christmas;
Sing, angel choirs! Let tills
ring out *Gloria* in the stores;
Mary and Joseph, banging
on doors

A CHRISTMAS CAROL

Come all ye faithful, ghosts
of playgrounds near and far,
sounds of swing and see-saw,
shufflings at the bar

Joyful and triumphant,
leather on willow;
A good innings, tears
on my pillow

Came ye to London town,
prostrate before Eros
on a single to
the Circus

one Christmas

WALKING THE DOG

Winter sun, like a lukewarm kiss
at homecoming. Candles in the trees
lit for memories once content
to snuggle at the breast,
now tugging at the leash, like
a setter after a mate - and it's getting late,
later than it should be for a walk
in the country at Christmas, seeking
any excuse to be somewhere else
than crackers and wine, hail-fellows-well-met
toasting times best forgot - through
a rose tinted haze of celebration
courtesy of Jesus Christ, who lived
and died - a man or more?
Let the arguments rage, as they do
at our own front door

And what on earth for?

You, me, and more to life than this
walking the dog each Christmas

CRISIS AT CHRISTMAS

Christmas, a special time of year;
Thoughts of home deserve a special tear;
Loneliness, greater than a fear
of nights and days; maze without end
it seems, in our worst waking dreams.
Whatever creed or need, hear a prayer
for the strength to endure, ways to be sure
that - for all our pain - such as we
will live, laugh, love again

Kisses flaunted on Queer Street;
one for each chair
left haunted
each year

Ah, Christmas! A dreamtime yearning
stirs the soul; hearts burning like mistakes
on the fire; flames risen higher and higher
as we pile on an agony of self-blame,
calling out in Someone's name to restore us,
cool and clean - to a world that need hang
its head in shame of us no more,
nor feed a Spiral of Madness
to heaven's door

Who to wipe our tears, calm
our fears, rewrite history - take us
proudly through a maze
of bigotry and hate?

Santa's running late

AN ULSTER CAROL

Peace on earth, goodwill to all
scratched in blood on a factory wall,
daily witness to the fears
of Ulster's men and women;
Suffer the children, come play
the horn - celebrate who's born
today, courtesy of the IRA;
Hark, the leafy vaults of spring!
A glove dropped in the market place
makes headline news in Dublin;
A butterfly shot down
over Washington

Dreaming of a decent job
instead of intimidation and loss
creeping across a land that's loved
even as the naming goes on
tit-for-tat and any occasion
to keep the feast on the front page
even when the appetite's gone;
So whose the stomach for cake
and wine at Stephen's wake?
(No friend of mine by the cock's
third throw!) Onward soldiers, go?
No fear, the gang's all here!

Silent night, holy night, amen.
Promises, promises - again, again!
Nothing new when morning breaks
but history and all it takes, to
murder the grass, kill the corn,
scare the children yet unborn,

light the candles. Double-speak
across congregations patiently
waiting for God to take a lead, made
to listen instead to the noisy feet
of would-be martyrs to graffiti
on Glove Street

(Belfast, 1994)

CHRISTMAS COMES BUT ONCE A YEAR, IF ONLY!

Another drink, they said.
No thanks, said I.
(Driving a friend, drew
the short straw);
Go on, can't do any harm;
No one likes a spoilsport.
(Drunk more beers than this,
I thought - no sweat).
So, one more for the road…
It's Christmas, nothing bad
can happen. O, but they lied!
Someone died, friend's
in a wheelchair

Life's a nightmare

ADVENT CALENDAR

Through a chink in the sky
glimpse a solitary star
wishing Christmas on me
where I sit alone
watching a ghostly pair
in the street below
embracing all the comfort and joy
that ever was, walk hand in hand
through Santa's Grotto
where light's but a stage
for rainbows, darkness no more
than its absence;
A minute's silence, pray
for lovers everywhere
made to run for cover
at Christmas;
Count the cards, who's missing?
Holier-than-thou mucking in
with token festivity, soon
has modern society
on a merry rout

Gays, first out

ABOUT THE POET:

R. N. Taber was born in December, 1945 and graduated from the University of Kent in Canterbury, 1973. A librarian by profession, he now lives in London and works on an occasional basis in information work. Most of the poems in this volume have appeared in various poetry magazines and anthologies in the U.K. and U.S.A. during 1993 - 2000; many were written much earlier. He writes a psycho-sociological poetry that views neither the gay world nor the world in general through rose tinted glasses. However, he describes himself as a positive thinker; a thread of optimism can be detected in even the most downbeat of his poems. He frequently experiments with voices. Although he often writes in the first person, many of his poems are a combination of observation, role-play and personal experience, exploring new ways of seeing and feeling. In 1996, a selection of his own gay-interest poems, *August and Genet,* was published under the auspices of Aramby Publications - WIRE Poetry Booklets (No.12). His work has been placed in several (U.K.) National Poetry competitions. The gay-interest poem, *Ordinary People,* won a 2nd prize in the Forward Press *Top 100 Poets* Competition, 1997-1998.

Your comments are always welcome. Write to Assembly Books at the address given or e-mail RogerTab@aol.com.

"No, I don't write gay poetry - just poetry. Poetry is poetry is poetry just as people are people are people. Colour, creed, sex, sexuality…these are but parts of a whole. It is the whole that counts."

Acknowledgements:

I would like to thank all those editors and publishers who have included my work in various poetry magazines/anthologies since I began submitting for publication in 1993. RNT